GRAMMAR
Form and Function

1A

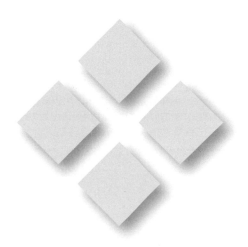

Milada Broukal

McGraw-Hill ESL/ELT

Grammar Form and Function 1A

Published by McGraw-Hill ESL/ELT, a business unit of The McGraw-Hill Companies,
Inc., 1221 Avenue of the Americas, New York, NY 10020. Copyright © 2004 by
The McGraw-Hill Companies, Inc. All rights reserved. No part of this publication may be
reproduced or distributed in any form or by any means, or stored in a database or retrieval
system, without the prior written consent of The McGraw-Hill Companies, Inc., including,
but not limited to, in any network or other electronic storage or transmission, or broadcast
for distance learning.

ISBN: 0-07-301195-9

Editorial director: Tina B. Carver
Senior managing editor: Erik Gundersen
Developmental editors: Arley Gray, Annie Sullivan
Editorial assistants: David Averbach, Kasey Williamson
Production managers: Alfonso Reyes, Juanita Thompson
Cover design: AcentoVisual
Interior design: AcentoVisual
Art: Alejando Benassini, Eldon Doty

Photo credits:
All photos are courtesy of Getty Images Royalty-Free Collection with the exception of the following:
Page 53 (left) Leonardo da Vinci/Getty Images, (right) © Bettmann/CORBIS; *Page 54* Portrait of
Wolfgang Amadeus Mozart (1756-91), Austrian composer/Johann Heinrich Wilhelm Tischbein/The
Bridgeman Art Library/Getty Images; *Page 159* © Karl Ammann/CORBIS.

McGraw-Hill ESL/ELT

Contents

UNIT 1 THE PRESENT TENSE OF *BE*

UNIT 2 *BE: IT, THERE,* AND THE PAST TENSE OF *BE*

UNIT 3 THE SIMPLE PRESENT TENSE

UNIT 4 THE PRESENT PROGRESSIVE TENSE

UNIT 5 NOUNS AND PRONOUNS

UNIT 6 THE SIMPLE PAST TENSE

UNIT 7 THE PAST PROGRESSIVE TENSE

APPENDICES

Acknowledgements

The publisher and author would like to thank the following individuals who reviewed *Grammar Form and Function* during the development of the series and whose comments and suggestions were invaluable in creating this project.

- ❖ Tony Albert, *Jewish Vocational Services, San Francisco, CA*
- ❖ Leslie A. Biaggi, *Miami–Dade Community College, Miami, FL*
- ❖ Gerry Boyd, *Northern Virginia Community College, VA*
- ❖ Marcia M. Captan, *Miami–Dade Community College, Miami, FL*
- ❖ Yongjae Paul Choe, *Dongguk University, Seoul, Korea*
- ❖ Sally Gearhart, *Santa Rosa Junior College, Santa Rosa, CA*
- ❖ Mary Gross, *Miramar College, San Diego, CA*
- ❖ Martin Guerin, *Miami–Dade Community College, Miami, FL*
- ❖ Patty Heiser, *University of Washington, Seattle, WA*
- ❖ Susan Kasten, *University of North Texas, Denton, TX*
- ❖ Sarah Kegley, *Georgia State University, Atlanta, GA*
- ❖ Kelly Kennedy-Isern, *Miami–Dade Community College, Miami, FL*
- ❖ Grace Low, *Germantown, TN*
- ❖ Irene Maksymjuk, *Boston University, Boston, MA*
- ❖ Christina Michaud, *Bunker Hill Community College, Boston, MA*
- ❖ Cristi Mitchell, *Miami–Dade Community College-Kendall Campus, Miami, FL*
- ❖ Carol Piñeiro, *Boston University, Boston, MA*
- ❖ Michelle Remaud, *Roxbury Community College, Boston, MA*
- ❖ Diana Renn, *Wentworth Institute of Technology, Boston, MA*
- ❖ Alice Savage, *North Harris College, Houston, TX*
- ❖ Karen Stanley, *Central Piedmont Community College, Charlotte, NC*
- ❖ Roberta Steinberg, *Mt. Ida College, Newton, MA*

The author would like to thank everyone at McGraw-Hill who participated in this project's development, especially Arley Gray, Erik Gundersen, Annie Sullivan, Jennifer Monaghan, David Averbach, Kasey Williamson, and Tina Carver.

Welcome to Grammar
Form and Function!

In **Grammar Form and Function 1**, high-interest photos bring beginning grammar to life, providing visual contexts for learning and retaining new structures and vocabulary.

Welcome to **Grammar Form and Function**. This visual tour will provide you with an overview of a unit from Book 1.

❖ *Form* presentations teach grammar structures through complete charts and memorable photos that facilitate students' recall of grammar structures.

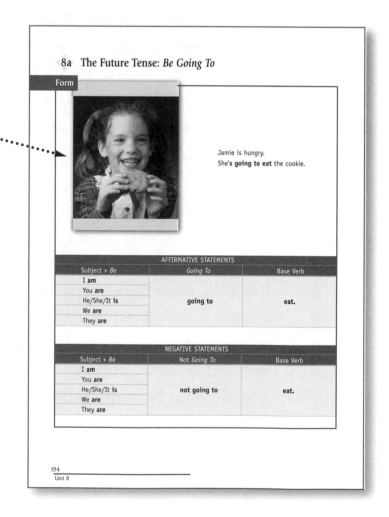

8a   The Future Tense: *Be Going To*

Form

Jamie is hungry.
She**'s going to eat** the cookie.

AFFIRMATIVE STATEMENTS		
Subject + *Be*	*Going To*	Base Verb
I **am**		
You **are**		
He/She/It **is**	**going to**	**eat.**
We **are**		
They **are**		

NEGATIVE STATEMENTS		
Subject + *Be*	Not *Going To*	Base Verb
I **am**		
You **are**		
He/She/It **is**	**not going to**	**eat.**
We **are**		
They **are**		

194
Unit 8

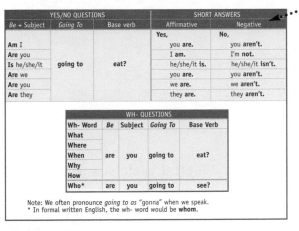

YES/NO QUESTIONS			SHORT ANSWERS	
Be + Subject	*Going To*	Base verb	Affirmative	Negative
Am I			**Yes,**	**No,**
Am I			you **are.**	you **aren't.**
Are you			I **am.**	I'm **not.**
Is he/she/it	going to	eat?	he/she/it **is.**	he/she/it **isn't.**
Are we			you **are.**	you **aren't.**
Are you			we **are.**	we **aren't.**
Are they			they **are.**	they **aren't.**

WH- QUESTIONS				
Wh- Word	*Be*	Subject	*Going To*	Base Verb
What				
Where				
When	are	you	going to	eat?
Why				
How				
Who*	are	you	going to	see?

Note: We often pronounce *going to* as "gonna" when we speak.
* In formal written English, the wh- word would be **whom.**

❖ *Form* **presentations** also include related grammatical points such as negatives, yes/no questions, wh– questions, and short answers.

Function

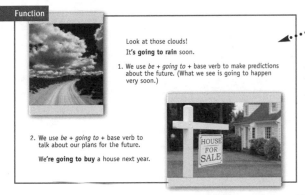

Look at those clouds!
It's **going to rain** soon.

1. We use *be + going to* + base verb to make predictions about the future. (What we see is going to happen very soon.)

2. We use *be + going to* + base verb to talk about our plans for the future.

   We're going to buy a house next year.

HOUSE FOR SALE

195
The Future Tense

❖ *Function* **explanations and examples** clarify when to use grammar structures.

---

1 Practice

Look at the photos. Then complete the sentences with *be going to* and a verb from the list.

buy some fruit
drink a cup of coffee
eat an ice cream cone

hit the ball
order a meal
paint the wall

pay the bill
take a photo
write a check

1. Jim has a camera.
Jim is going to take a photo .

2. Brad has a paintbrush.
_____ .

3. Sue is in the supermarket.
_____ .

4. Tony is in a café.
_____ .

5. Mel has a checkbook and a pen.
_____ .

6. Ted is in a restaurant.
_____ .

196
Unit 8

❖ **Extensive practice** guides students from accurate production to fluent use of the grammar.

❖ **High-interest photos** contextualize the grammar and provide visual cues in practice exercises.

11 Practice

Make predictions for the year 2050. Say what you think. Use *will or won't* in the blanks.

1. People _____*will*_____ drive electric cars.
2. Everybody _____ have a computer at home.
3. People _____ carry money.
4. People _____ take vacations on the moon.
5. All people _____ speak the same language.
6. All people around the world _____ use the same currency (money).
7. People _____ find life on other planets.
8. People _____ get serious diseases like cancer.
9. Trains _____ travel very fast.
10. People _____ live to be 130 years old.
11. Men and women _____ continue to marry.
12. Children _____ go to school five days a week.

Discuss with your partner or the class.
Write three sentences with *will or won't* about what you think will happen.

12 Practice

Complete the conversation with forms of the present progressive, *will,* and *be going to.*

Julia: I (go) _____*am going*_____ to the supermarket right now. Do you want anything?
              1

Leyla: Yes. Can you get some orange juice?

Julia: Sure. It's on my list, so I (get) _____ it.
                                               2

Leyla: I also wanted to pick up my photos today, but I don't have time to do it.

Julia: Don't worry. I (pick) _____ them up for you. I
                               3

    (be) _____ back soon. (be) _____ you _____ here?
           4   5   6

Leyla: I (go) _____ to work now.
               7

Julia: OK. I (see) _____ you later. Remember Tony and Suzy
                     8

    (come) _____ tonight.
            9

❖ **Topical exercises** provide opportunities for students to use grammar naturally.

9 Practice

Complete the dialogue. Use the present progressive of the verbs in parentheses.

Mike: What (do) _*are*_ you _____*doing*_____ this weekend?
                   1   2

Jackie: Well, I'm really very busy. Tonight I (go) _____ out to dinner with
                                                  3

    my friend Lulu. She's great fun. We always have a good time. Then on Saturday

    morning I (take) _____ a computer class.
                     4

Mike: Finally! You're learning to use a computer!

Jackie: Yes, I love it. I'm doing well, too. Then, after that, I (meet) _____
                                                                      5

    my mother. We (go) _____ shopping to get my father a birthday gift.
                       6

    Then, in the evening, I (have)_____ dinner with Chris. On Sunday,
                                  7

    Chris and I (go) _____ to a friend's wedding. So on Sunday morning,
                     8

    I (get) _____ dressed, and he (pick) _____ me up to
            9   10

    go there. He (drive) _____ there. It's a long drive. We
                         11

    (stay) _____ there for the dinner reception then we
           12

    (come) _____ back at around six. Chris (fly) _____
            13   14

    to Boston in the evening, and I (go) _____ over to Magda's place
                                         15

    to study English. You know we (have) _____ a test on Monday.
                                          16

    So anyway, Mike, what (do) _____ you _____?
                               17   18

Mike: Oh, nothing really.

Jackie: My bus is here. See you Monday! Bye!

10 Your Turn

Work with a partner. Ask and answer the questions.

Example:
You: Where are you going after class?
Your partner: I'm going home.

Today	Tomorrow	On the weekend
where/go/after class	what/do/tomorrow	where/go/Saturday
how/get/there	where/go/evening	what/do/Sunday
what/do/this evening		

❖ **Your Turn** activities guide students to practice grammar in personally meaningful conversations.

❖ **Writing assignments** build composition skills, such as narrating and describing, through real-life, step-by-step tasks.

WRITING: Describe Future Plans

Write a paragraph about future plans.

Step 1. Work with a partner. A friend is coming to your town/city for three days. It is his/her first visit. Make a list of four good places to go.

1. _____   3. _____

2. _____   4. _____

Step 2. Plan your three days. Where are you going to go first, second, third, and last? Your friend is arriving at 4:00 at the airport near your town. Ask your partner questions like these. Write the answers to the questions.

1. Are you going to meet your friend at the airport?
2. Where are you going to take him/her after that?
3. What are you going to do that evening? Why?
4. What are you going to do on Saturday?
5. What are you going to do if the weather is bad?
6. What will you do on Sunday?
7. How will you get there?
8. What special food will you give your friend to eat?

SELF-TEST

A Choose the best answer, A, B, C, or D, to complete the sentence. Mark your answer by darkening the oval with the same letter.

1. When I go to London, I _____ Buckingham Palace.

   A. am visiting   Ⓐ Ⓑ Ⓒ Ⓓ
   B. going visit
   C. am going to visit
   D. will visiting

2. What _____ on the weekend?

   A. are you going to do
   B. are you going   Ⓐ Ⓑ Ⓒ Ⓓ
   C. you are going to do
   D. you doing

6. In twenty years, most people _____ electric cars.

   A. are driving   Ⓐ Ⓑ Ⓒ Ⓓ
   B. will drive
   C. going drive
   D. is going to drive

7. I will be worried before I _____ to the interview.

   A. will go   Ⓐ Ⓑ Ⓒ Ⓓ
   B. go
   C. am going

❖ **Self-Tests** at the end of each unit allow students to evaluate their mastery of the grammar while providing informal practice of standardized test taking.

B Find the underlined word or phrase, A, B, C, or D, that is incorrect. Mark your answer by darkening the oval with the same letter.

1. How will be jobs different in the future?
     A   B   C   D

   Ⓐ Ⓑ Ⓒ Ⓓ

6. In the future, men and women will be
              A   B   C

   continue to marry.
    D

   Ⓐ Ⓑ Ⓒ Ⓓ

2. In the United States, you leave a tip
                  A

   when you having dinner in a restaurant.
        B   C   D

   Ⓐ Ⓑ Ⓒ Ⓓ

7. If sharks do not move all the time, they
          A B   C

   will be die.
    D

   Ⓐ Ⓑ Ⓒ Ⓓ

To the Teacher

Grammar Form and Function is a three-level series designed to ensure students' success in learning grammar. The series features interesting photos to help students accurately recall grammar points, meaningful contexts, and a clear, easy-to-understand format that integrates practice of the rules of essential English grammar (form) with information about when to apply them and what they mean (function).

Features

* ❖ **Flexible approach to grammar instruction** integrates study of new structures (form) with information on how to use them and what they mean (function).
* ❖ **High-interest photos** contextualize new grammar and vocabulary.
* ❖ **Comprehensive grammar coverage** targets all important structures.
* ❖ **Extensive practice** ensures accurate production and fluent use of grammar.
* ❖ **Your Turn activities** guide students to practice grammar in personally meaningful conversations.
* ❖ **Writing assignments** build composition skills like narrating and describing through step-by-step tasks.
* ❖ **Self-Tests and Unit Quizzes** offer multiple assessment tools for student and teacher use, in print and Web formats.
* ❖ **Companion Website activities** develop real-world listening skills.

Components

* ❖ **Student Book** has 14 units with abundant practice in both form and function of each grammar structure. Each unit also features communicative *Your Turn* activities, a step-by-step *Writing* assignment, and a *Self-Test*.
* ❖ **Teacher's Manual** provides the following:
  * ◆ Teaching tips and techniques
  * ◆ Overview of each unit
  * ◆ Answer keys for the Student Book and Workbook
  * ◆ Expansion activities
  * ◆ Culture, usage, and vocabulary notes
  * ◆ Answers to frequently asked questions about the grammar structures
  * ◆ Unit quizzes in a standardized test format and answer keys for each quiz.
* ❖ **Workbook** features additional exercises for each grammar structure, plus an extra student Self-Test at the end of each unit.
* ❖ **Website** provides further practice, as well as expansion opportunities for students.

Overview of the Series

Pedagogical Approach

What is *form*?

Form is the structure of a grammar point and what it looks like. Practice of the form builds students' accuracy and helps them recognize the grammar point in authentic situations, so they are better prepared to understand what they are reading or what other people are saying.

What is *function*?

Function is when and how we use a grammar point. Practice of the function builds students' fluency and helps them apply the grammar point in their real lives.

Why does **Grammar Form and Function** incorporate both form and function into its approach to teaching grammar?

Mastery of grammar relies on students knowing the rules of English (form) and correctly understanding how to apply them (function). Providing abundant practice in both form and function is key to student success.

How does **Grammar Form and Function** incorporate form and function into its approach to teaching grammar?

For each grammar point, the text follows a consistent format:

❖ **Presentation of Form.** The text presents the complete form, or formal rule, along with several examples for students to clearly see the model. There are also relevant photos to help illustrate the grammar point.

❖ **Presentation of Function.** The text explains the function of the grammar point, or how it is used, along with additional examples for reinforcement.

❖ **Practice.** Diverse exercises practice the form and function together. Practice moves logically from more controlled to less controlled activities.

❖ **Application.** Students apply the grammar point in open-ended communicative activities. **Your Turn** requires students to draw from and speak about personal experiences, and **Writing** provides a variety of writing assignments that rely on communicative group and pair discussions. **Expansion** activities in the Teacher's Manual provide additional creative, fun practice for students.

What is the purpose of the photos in the book?

Most people have a visual memory. When you see a photo aligned with a grammar point, the photo helps you remember and contextualize the grammar. The photo reinforces the learning and retention. If there were no visual image, you'd be more likely to forget the grammar point. For example, let's say you are learning the present progressive. You read the example "She is drinking a glass of water." At the same time, you are shown a photo of a girl drinking a glass of water. Later, you are more likely to recall the form of the present progressive because your mind has made a mental picture that helps you remember.

Practice

How were the grammar points selected?

We did a comprehensive review of courses at this level to ensure that all of the grammar points taught were included.

Does **Grammar Form and Function** have controlled or communicative practice?

It has both. Students practice each grammar point through controlled exercises and then move on to tackle open-ended communicative activities.

Do students have a chance to personalize the grammar?

Yes. There are opportunities to personalize the grammar in **Your Turn** and **Writing**. **Your Turn** requires students to draw from and speak about personal experiences, and **Writing** provides a variety of writing assignments that rely on communicative group and pair discussions.

Does **Grammar Form and Function** help students work toward fluency or accuracy?

Both. The exercises are purposefully designed to increase students' accuracy and enhance their fluency by practicing both form and function. Students' confidence in their accuracy helps boost their fluency.

Why does the text feature writing practice?

Grammar and writing are linked in a natural way. Specific grammar structures lend themselves to specific writing genres. In *Grammar Form and Function*, carefully devised practice helps students keep these structures in mind as they are writing.

In addition to the grammar charts, what other learning aids are in the book?

The book includes 19 pages of appendices that are designed to help the students as they complete the exercises. In addition to grammar resources such as lists of irregular verbs and spelling rules for endings, the appendices also feature useful and interesting information, including grammar terms, rules for capitalization and punctuation, writing basics, and even maps. In effect, the appendices constitute a handbook that students can use not only in grammar class, but in other classes as well.

Are there any additional practice opportunities?

Yes, there are additional exercises in the Workbook and on the Website. There are also **Expansion** activities in the Teacher's Manual that provide more open-ended (and fun!) practice for students.

Assessment

What is the role of student self-assessment in **Grammar Form and Function?**

Every opportunity for student self-assessment is valuable! *Grammar Form and Function* provides two Self-Tests for each unit – one at the end of each Student Book unit and another at the end of each Workbook unit. The Self-Tests build student confidence, encourage student independence as learners, and increase student competence in following standardized test formats. In addition, the Self-Tests serve as important tools for the teacher in measuring student mastery of grammar structures.

Does **Grammar Form and Function** offer students practice in standardized test formats?

Yes, the two Self-Tests and the Unit Quiz for each unit all utilize standardized test formats. Teachers may use the three tests in the way that best meets student, teacher, and institutional needs. For example, teachers may first assign the Self-Test in the Workbook as an untimed practice test to be taken at home. Then in the classroom, teachers may administer the Self-Test in the Student Book for a more realistic, but still informal, test-taking experience. Finally, teachers may administer the Unit Quiz from the Teacher's Manual as a more standardized timed test.

How long should each Self-Test or Unit Quiz take?

Since there is flexibility in implementing the Self-Tests and Unit Quizzes, there is also flexibility in the timing of the tests. When used for informal test-taking practice at home or in class, they may be administered as untimed tests. When administered as timed tests in class, they should take no more than 20 minutes.

How can I be sure students have mastered the grammar?

Grammar Form and Function provides a variety of tools to evaluate student mastery of the grammar. Traditional evaluation tools include the practice exercises, Self-Tests, and Unit Quizzes. To present a more complete picture of student mastery, the series also includes **Your Turn** activities and **Writing**, which illustrate how well students have internalized the grammar structures and are able to apply them in realistic tasks. Teachers can use these activities to monitor and assess students' ability to incorporate new grammatical structures into their spoken and written discourse.

Unit Format

What is the unit structure of **Grammar Form and Function**?

Consult the guide to **Grammar Form and Function** on pages VIII-XI. This walk-through provides a visual tour of a Student Book unit.

How many hours of instruction are in **Grammar Form and Function 1**?

The key to **Grammar Form and Function** is flexibility! The grammar structures in the Student Book may be taught in order, or teachers may rearrange units into an order that best meets their students' needs. To shorten the number of hours of instruction, teachers may choose not to teach all of the grammar structures, or use all of the exercises provided. On the other hand, teachers may add additional hours by assigning exercises in the Workbook or on the Website. In addition, the Teacher's Manual provides teaching suggestions and expansion activities that would add extra hours of instruction.

Ancillary Components

What can I find in the Teacher's Manual?

❖ Teaching tips and techniques
❖ Overview of each unit
❖ Answer keys for the Student Book and Workbook
❖ Expansion activities
❖ Culture, usage, and vocabulary notes
❖ Answers to frequently asked questions about the grammar structures
❖ Unit quizzes in a standardized test format and quiz answer keys.

How do I supplement classroom instruction with the Workbook?

The Workbook exercises can be used to add instructional hours to the course, to provide homework practice, and to reinforce and refresh the skills of students who have mastered the grammar structures. It also provides additional standardized test-taking practice.

What can students find on the Website?

Students and teachers will find a wealth of engaging listening and reading activities on the **Grammar Form and Function** Website. As with the Workbook, the Website exercises can be used to add instructional hours to the course, to provide homework practice, and to reinforce and refresh the skills of students who have mastered the grammar structures.

UNIT 1

THE PRESENT TENSE OF *BE*

1a Nouns: Singular **(a book)**

1b Nouns: Plural **(books)**

1c Subject Pronouns **(I, you, he, she, it, we, they)**

1d Subject Pronoun + Present Tense of *Be* **(I am, I'm)**

1e Negative of *Be* **(I am not. I'm not.)**

1f *Be* + Adjective **(I'm happy.)**

1g Possessive Adjectives **(my, your, his, her, its, our, their)**

1h Demonstrative Adjectives **(this/that, these/those)**

1i Yes/No Questions with *Be* **(Are you a student? Is she a student?)**

1j Questions with *What, Where,* and *Who*

1k Prepositions of Place **(in, on, under, above, between)**

❖ Writing

❖ Self-Test

1a Nouns: Singular

Nouns name people, places, animals, and things.

dog   apple   boy

Nouns can be singular (one) or plural (more than one).
We put *a* or *an* in front of many singular nouns.
A and *an* have the same meaning. They mean one (1).

1. We use *an* when a word begins with the vowels *a, e, i,* and *o.*
    an apple   **an** egg   **an** ice cream   **an** orange
    We use *an* when a word begins with "u" and has a vowel sound .
    an umbrella   **an** uncle
    But we use *a* when a word begins with the vowel "u" and sounds like "y."
    a university   **a** united country   **a** unit

2. We also use *an* when a word begins with a silent "h."
    an hour   **an** honest man   **an** honorable person
    But we use *a* when the "h" is not silent.
    a house   **a** horse   **a** hat

3. We use *a* when a word begins with a consonant sound: *b, c, d, f, k, l, t, w, y,* and so forth.
    a book   **a** teacher   **a** country   **a** cat   **a** flower

Put _a_ or _an_ before the word.

1. ___a___ table
2. _____ ear
3. _____ animal
4. _____ hotel
5. _____ eye
6. _____ armchair
7. _____ question
8. _____ uncle
9. _____ city
10. _____ house
11. _____ bed
12. _____ exercise
13. _____ university
14. _____ elephant
15. _____ office
16. _____ fish

1b Nouns: Plural

Form

| a boy | boys | a man | men |

Regular Plurals

Noun Ending	Spelling Rule	Examples	
		Singular (1)	Plural (1+)
Most consonants	Add **–s**	**a** book	book**s**
		a car	car**s**
		a teacher	teacher**s**
The consonants **s, ss, sh, ch, x**	Add **–es**	**a** bus	bus**es**
		a dress	dress**es**
		a dish	dish**es**
		a watch	watch**es**
		a box	box**es**

Regular Plurals			
Noun Ending	Spelling Rule	Examples	
		Singular (1)	Plural (1+)
Consonant + **y**	Drop **y** add **-ies**	**a** baby	bab**ies**
		a country	countr**ies**
Vowel + **y**	Add **s**	**a** boy	boy**s**
f or **fe**	Change to **–ves**	**a** knife	kni**ves**
		a life	li**ves**

Irregular Plurals

Singular	Plural
a man	m**e**n
a woman	wom**e**n
a child	child**ren**
a tooth	te**e**th
a foot	f**ee**t
a mouse	m**i**ce
a sheep	**sheep**
a fish	**fish**

We do not use **a/an** in the plural.

2 Practice

Give the plural.

1. key   _keys_

2. child   _____

3. city   _____

4. wife   _____

5. woman   _____

6. pen   _____

7. leaf   _____

8. mouse   _____

9. fish   _____

10. story   _____

11. foot   _____

12. lemon   _____

13. toy   _____

14. house   _____

15. sandwich   _____

16. doctor   _____

17. dictionary   _____

18. family   _____

19. brush   _____

20. match   _____

Practice

Read the words in the list. Write the plural form of them in the correct column.

chair	class	lady	pen	wife
child	fish	library	shelf	wolf
church	glass	party	street	woman

-s	-es	-ies	-ves	irregular
chairs	*classes*	*ladies*	*wolves*	*children*

1c Subject Pronouns

Form

Singular	Plural
I	we
you	you
he/she/it	they

Function

1. We use *he* for a man or a boy.

2. We use *she* for a woman or a girl.

3. We use *it* for an animal or a thing.

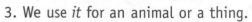

4. We use *they* for the plural. We use *they* for people, animals, and things.

Practice

Put *he, she, it,* or *they* under the pictures.

1. _____they_____

2. _____

3. _____

4. _____

5. _____

6. _____

7. _____

8. _____

9. _____

Practice

Complete with *he, she, it, we, you,* or *they.*

1. man	_____he_____	
2. woman	_____	
3. girls	_____	
4. chairs	_____	
5. dictionary	_____	
6. Tony and Ed	_____	
7. car	_____	
8. pen	_____	

9. cats	_____
10. book	_____
11. Susan and I	_____
12. boy	_____
13. Tony and you	_____
14. Kim and Lee	_____
15. Susan	_____
16. George	_____

1d Subject Pronoun + Present Tense of *Be*

Form

She's Annie. **He's** Eddy.
They are students.
They're Brazilian.

Pronoun + *Be*			Contractions
I	**am**	a student.	**I'm** a student.
You	**are**	a student.	**You're** a student.
He	**is**	Eddy.	**He's** Eddy.
She	**is**	Annie.	**She's** Annie.
It	**is**	a book.	**It's** a book.
We	**are**	students.	**We're** students.
You	**are**	friends.	**You're** friends.
They	**are**	Brazilian.	**They're** Brazilian.

We use *am, is,* and *are*:

1. To say who we are.
   I **am** Annie.   He**'s** Eddy.
2. To say what we are.
   We **are** students. They **are** teachers.
3. To talk about nationality.
   I**'m** Turkish.   They**'re** Brazilian.
4. To describe people, things, or places.
   He**'s** hungry.   She**'s** beautiful.

6 | Practice

Complete the sentences. Use *am, is,* or *are*.

1. I _____ *am* _____ a student.

2. You _____ a student too.

3. We _____ students.

4. He _____ a teacher.

5. Mr. Long and Mr. Black _____ teachers.

6. Annie _____ from Brazil.

7. Eddy _____ 16.

8. They _____ students.

9. You two _____ American.

10. She _____ from Singapore.

7 | Practice

Complete the sentence with contractions of *am, is,* or *are*.

1. It '*s* _____ a passport.

2. They _____ keys.

3. We _____ from Canada.

4. He _____ a doctor.

5. She _____ a teacher.

6. I _____ Italian.

7. You _____ late.

8. We _____ from Brazil.

9. It _____ a book.

10. He _____ from Spain.

1e Negative of *Be*

She **isn't** a student.
She**'s** a teacher.

Subject	Be + Not		Contractions with Subject	Contractions with *Not*
I	**am not**	a teacher.	**I'm not** a teacher.	*
You	**are not**	from Mexico.	**You're not** from Mexico.	you **aren't**
He		a student.	**He's not** a student.	he **isn't**
She	**is not**	21.	**She's not** 21.	she **isn't**
It		good.	**It's not** good.	it **isn't**
We		Americans.	**We're not** Americans.	we **aren't**
You	**are not**	teachers.	**You're not** teachers.	you **aren't**
They		from Japan.	**They're not** from Japan.	they **aren't**

* There is no contraction for *am not*.

8 Practice

Complete the sentences. Use the long form of the negative *(am not, is not, are not)*.

1. Mexico _____*is not*_____ a city. It's a country.

2. I _____ Spanish. I'm Italian.

3. You _____ Spanish.

4. He _____ from China. He's from Korea.

5. She _____ from Brazil. She's from Venezuela.

6. We _____ from Hong Kong. We're from Singapore.

7. They _____ from England. They're from Australia.

8. It _____ from China. It's from Japan.

9. My parents _____ here. They're in Taiwan.

10. The teacher _____ from the United States. He's from Canada.

9 Practice

Complete the sentences with negative contractions (*'s not, isn't,* etc.).

1. I 'm not _____ in Class 1A. I'm in Class 2A.

2. The class _____ at 10:00 It's at 9:00.

3. The students _____ in the classroom. They're outside.

4. The book _____ black. It's white.

5. The exercises _____ long. They're short.

6. The questions _____ difficult. They're easy.

7. She_____ in class today. She's sick.

8. The food in the cafeteria _____ bad. It's good.

9. I _____ ready. Please wait.

10. We're students. We _____ teachers.

10 Practice

Look at the chart below. Then complete the sentences with *is/isn't* or *are/aren't*.

Name	Country	Age	Occupation
Mei	China	28	teacher
Rengin	Turkey	26	student
Eduardo	Mexico	30	doctor
Nuri	Turkey	24	student

1. Mei ____is____ from China. She ____isn't____ from Turkey.

2. Mei _____ 28 years old. She _____ teacher.

3. Rengin _____ from Turkey. She _____ a doctor.

4. She _____ a student. She _____ 26 years old.

5. Eduardo _____ from Italy. He _____ from Mexico.

6. Eduardo _____ a doctor. He _____ a student.

7. Rengin and Nuri _____ from Turkey. They _____ students.

8. They _____ teachers. They _____ doctors.

| 11 | Your Turn |

Tell a partner about yourself. Make positive and negative statements. Give your name, occupation, and where you are from.

Example:
I'm Tom.
I'm not from Korea. I'm from Japan.
I'm not a doctor. I'm a student.

1f   *Be* + Adjective

Form

They are **young**.
They are **happy**.
They are **cute**.

Subject	*Be (Not)*	Adjective
A lemon	is	yellow.
Lemons	are	yellow.
A giraffe	is	tall.
Giraffes	are	tall.
Danny	is	happy.
They	are	happy.

1. Adjectives describe people or things.

    an **old** shoe   a **small** skirt   a **young** woman

    a **rich** family   a **cheap** ticket

2. Adjectives do not change for singular and plural.

    He is a **good** man.   They are three **good** women.

3. We can put an adjective after *be*.

    They are **hungry**.   We are **thirsty**.

4. We usually make adjectives of nationality from the name of the country.
    We write the country and the adjective with a capital letter.

    He is from **Turkey**.   He is **Turkish**.

Country	Adjective
Brazil	Brazilian
China	Chinese
Chile	Chilean
England	English
France	French
Iran	Iranian
Japan	Japanese
Korea	Korean
Mexico	Mexican
Norway	Norwegian
Peru	Peruvian
Poland	Polish
Portugal	Portuguese
Singapore	Singaporean
Sudan	Sudanese
Sweden	Swedish
Thailand	Thai
United States of America	American

12 Practice

Write sentences about the photos using adjectives from the list. Use *he, she, they,* and the present tense of *be*.

angry   happy   old   sad   strong   young

1. *She is sad* _____.

2. _____.

3. _____.

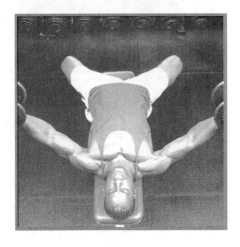

4. _____.

5. _____.

6. _____.

13 Practice

Complete the sentence with *is* or *are* and one of the adjectives from the list. More then one answer is possible.

brown	fresh	hot	sour
chewy	green	red	spicy
cold	hard	salty	sweet
crunchy	heavy	soft	white

1. A lemon *is sour* _____.

2. Tomatoes _____.

3. Eggs _____.

4. Potato chips _____.

5. A watermelon _____.

6. An ice cube _____.

7. An apple _____.

8. Sugar _____.

9. Cakes _____.

10. Soup _____.

11. Bread _____.

12. Carrot sticks _____.

13. Broccoli _____.

14. Chocolate _____.

15. Bubble gum _____.

16. Peppers _____.

The Present Tense of *Be*

14 Practice

Complete the sentences with an affirmative or negative contraction of *be* and an adjective from the list.

happy   lazy   shy   sick
heavy   rich   short   single

Ted

1. Ted isn't poor. He *is rich* _____.

2. Ted isn't tall. He _____.

3. Ted isn't sad. He _____.

4. Ted is friendly. He _____.

5. He is healthy. He _____.

6. He isn't married. He _____.

7. He isn't hardworking. He _____.

8. Ted isn't thin. He _____.

Practice

Look at the picture of Ann. Write sentences using *is/isn't* or *are/aren't* and one of the adjectives in parentheses.

Name: Ann Greene
Nationality: American
Marital Status: Single
Occupation: University student
Height: 6 feet (1.8 meters)
Weight: 143 pounds (65 kilos)

Ann

1. (Chinese/American) *She isn't Chinese. She's American*   ,

2. (tall/short) _____.

3. (hardworking/lazy) _____.

4. (heavy/slim) _____.

5. (young/old) _____.

6. (single/married) _____.

16 Your Turn

Talk about yourself. Use five adjectives from the list.

friendly/shy   hardworking/lazy   married/single   tall/short   young/old

Example:
My name is Elsie Gonzalez. I'm hardworking. I'm friendly.

1g Possessive Adjectives

Form

That's **my** teacher.

Her name is Ms. Bell.

Pronouns	Possessive Adjectives
I	**my**
you	**your**
he	**his**
she	**her**
it	**its**
we	**our**
they	**their**

Function

We call *my, your, his, her, its, our,* and *their* possessive adjectives. We use possessive adjectives before nouns.

my book   **his** name   **our** house

We use possessive adjectives to show that something belongs to someone.

My car is red.   **Her** car is blue.

17 Practice

Complete the sentences with *my, your, his, her, its, our,* **or** *their.*

I have a brother. _____My_____ brother is married. _____ wife is a
                            1   2
teacher. They have a baby. _____ baby is six months old. The baby is a girl.
                                    3
_____ name is Maria. I have a sister, too. _____ name is Sandra.
        4   5
She is married, too. _____ husband's name is Tony. They have a boy.
                            6

_____ name is Alex. _____ brother and sister are not in this country.
                 7   **8**
They are in Mexico. You say you have a brother and a sister. _____ brother and
                                                                               9
sister are married, too. _____ brother is in Korea, but _____ sister is
                                10   **11**
in this city. You are lucky!

18 Practice

Anita is talking about her family. Complete the sentences with *my, your, his, her, its,*
our, **or** *their.*

_____My_____ name is Anita. I'm 20 years old. I am a student.
         1
_____ brother is a student, too. _____ name is Andrew.
    2   **3**
He is _____ favorite brother. I have a mother and a father. They are in
          4
Los Angeles. _____ last name is Armstrong. _____ father is 53 years
                    5   **6**
old. _____ name is Robert. _____ mother is 48 years old.
        7   **8**
_____ name is Olivia. They have a house. _____ house is small.
    9   **10**
They also have a cat. _____ name is Spot. I have four brothers and two sisters.
                            11
We have a big family. _____ family is big and happy!
                            12

19 Your Turn

Look at the chart and talk about Anita, Andrew, their parents, and you.
Use *his, her, their,* **and** *my.*

	Music	Sports	Food
Anita	rock	tennis	chocolate
Andrew	rock	football	French fries
Their Parents	opera	ice-skating	pasta
You	*jazz*		

Example:
Her favorite music is rock.
Her favorite sport is tennis.

1h Demonstrative Adjectives

Ray: Look at **this** photo!

Joanne: **That**'s Venice. **Those** are gondolas!

Singular	Plural
this book	**these** books
that book	**those** books

Function

We use *this* and *these* for people and things that are near to us. We use *that* and *those* for people and things that are not near.

This is my book. (The book is near me.)
That is your book. (The book is not near me.)

20 Practice

Mrs. Cooper has a visitor. Her name is Berta. Berta wants to practice her English.
Complete Berta's answers with *this is, that is, these are,* or *those are*.

Mrs. Cooper: Give me the English names for the things you can see.

Berta: **1.** _This is_ a table.

       2. _____ a newspaper.

       3. _____ a dictionary.

       4. _____ clouds.

       5. _____ a horse.

       6. _____ a pen.

       7. _____ a cup.

       8. _____ cows.

       9. _____ sandwiches.

     10. _____ mountains.

     11. _____ a napkin.

     12. _____ trees.

21 Your Turn

Point to or touch things or people in the classroom. Use *this* and *that*.

blackboard	classmate	jacket	teacher
chair	dictionary	notebook	watch

Example:
This is my jacket.

1i Yes/No Questions with *Be*

Are you from Indonesia?
No, we're not.
We're from India.

YES/NO QUESTIONS			SHORT ANSWERS	
Be	Subject		Affirmative	Negative
			Yes,	**No,**
Am	I		you **are.**	you**'re not**/you **aren't.**
Are	you		I **am.**	I**'m not.**
Is	he	from India?	he **is.**	he**'s not**/he **isn't.**
	she		she **is.**	she**'s not**/she **isn't.**
	it		it **is.**	it**'s not**/it **isn't.**
Are	you		we **are.**	we**'re not**/we **aren't.**
	we		you **are.**	you**'re not**/you **aren't.**
	they		they **are.**	they**'re not**/they **aren't.**

1. Yes/no questions begin with *am, is,* or *are*. In short answers we only use *yes* or *no*, the subject pronoun, and the verb. We add *not* if the answer is negative.

   Are you a student? **Yes I am. / No, I'm not.**

2. After *yes*, we do not contract forms of *be*. After *no*, there are two possible contractions. There is no difference in meaning.

   It **isn't** here. OR It**'s not** here.

   CORRECT: Yes, **I am.** / Yes, **she is.**
   INCORRECT: ~~Yes, I'm.~~ / ~~Yes, she's.~~

---

22 Practice

Read the information about the two people below. Then complete the questions and answers.

Name:	Patricia Carlos
Age:	19
Job:	Student
Nationality:	Colombian
Marital Status:	Single

Name:	Dave Fan
Age:	18
Job:	Student
Nationality:	Malaysian
Marital Status:	Single

Questions	**Answers**
1. <u>Is she</u> a teacher?	No, she isn't.
2. Is she young?	Yes, <u>she is</u>.
3. Is she Brazilian?	No, _____.
4. _____ Colombian?	Yes, she is.
5. _____ 19 years old?	Yes, she is.
6. Is she a student?	Yes, _____.
7. _____ 19 years old?	No, he isn't.
8. _____ Malaysian?	Yes, he is.
9. Is he a doctor?	No, _____.
10. _____ single?	Yes, he is.
11. _____ students?	Yes, they are.
12. _____ young?	Yes, they are.
13. Are they single?	Yes, _____.
14. _____ American?	No, they aren't.

23 Practice

Ask questions and give answers.

1. <u>Is she</u> a teacher?
   <u>No, she isn't.</u>
   <u>She's a doctor.</u>

2. <u>Are they</u> flowers?
   <u>Yes, they are.</u>
   _____

3. _____ a dog?

_____

_____

4. _____ a camera?

_____

_____

5. _____ books?

_____

_____

6. _____ glasses?

_____

_____

7. _____ peppers?

_____

_____

8. _____ the Statue of Liberty?

_____

_____

24 **Your Turn**

Ask your partner yes/no questions. Use the words below or add your own.

married   Mexican/Korean (any nationality)   student   young   20/23 (any age)

Example:
Are you Japanese?   Yes, I am.   OR   No, I'm not. I'm Korean.

lj ◆ Questions with *What, Where,* and *Who*

John: **Who** is she?

Sue: She is a student.

John: **What's** her name?

Sue: Her name is Maria Verdi.

John: **Where's** she from?

Sue: She's from Italy.

QUESTIONS			ANSWERS
Wh- Word	*Be*	Subject	
What	**is**	your name?	My name is Kelly.
What	**are**	these?	They're pens.
Where	**is**	Joe?	He's at home.
Where	**are**	you from?	I'm from Mexico.
Who	**is**	he?	He's my brother.
Who	**are**	they?	They're visitors.

Function

We use question words such as *what, where,* and *who* to ask for information.

1. We use *what* to ask questions about things.

   Question: **What** is that?

   Answer: It's a pen.

2. We use *where* to ask questions about location.

   Question: **Where** is Sylvia?

   Answer: She's at school.

3. We use *who* to ask questions about people.

   Question: **Who** is he?

   Answer: He's my teacher.

Contractions	
what is	**what's**
where is	**where's**
who is	**who's**

25 Practice

Match the questions in Column A with the answers in Column B.

	A		**B**
_c_	**1.** What's your name?		a. It's a book.
_____	**2.** Where are you from?		b. He's my father.
_____	**3.** Where are your parents?		c. My name is Norma Santos.
_____	**4.** Who is that woman?		d. They're in Mexico.
_____	**5.** What is it?		e. I'm from Mexico City.
_____	**6.** Who is he?		f. She's my teacher.

26 Practice

Look at the photos and the information about the people. Write questions with *who*, *what*, and *where*.

1. <u>Who is she</u>_____?

She is Sarah Jones.

2. _____?

She is an actress.

3. _____?

She is from New York.

4. _____?

He is Paul Estrada.

5. _____?

He is from Peru.

6. _____?

He is a student.

7. _____?

I'm Ben Thomas.

8. _____?

I'm from Canada.

9. _____?

I'm a teacher.

1k Prepositions of Place

We use prepositions of place to say where people or things are.
Here are some prepositions of place.

1. The mouse is **in** the box.

2. The mouse is **on** the box

3. The mouse is **under** the box.

4. The mouse is **behind** the box.

5. The mouse is **above** the box.

6. The mouse is **in front of** the box.

7. The mouse is **between** the boxes.

8. The mouse is **next to** the box.

We also say:
at school, **at** the office, **at** the airport
in my apartment, **in** the classroom
on the second floor, **on** the third floor, **on** the tenth floor

28

27 Practice

Complete the paragraph with prepositions from the list.

above
at
behind
in
in front of
next to
on
under

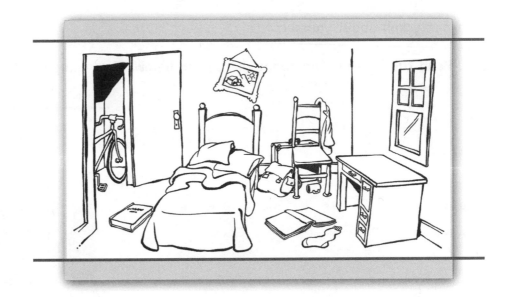

Ricky isn't _____*in*_____ his bedroom. He is _____ school
                  1   2
right now. His bedroom is _____ the second floor of his house. Look at his
                                    3
bedroom! A cup is _____ the chair. The picture is _____
                          4   5
the bed. His bicycle is _____ the closet. Books are _____
                                6   7
the floor. A desk is _____ the window. The suitcase is
                            8
_____ the chair. The backpack is _____ a chair.
        9   10

28 Your Turn

Work with a partner. Ask and answer questions with *where* and words from the list.

the board   the door   your backpack   your pen
the clock   the teacher   your book

Example:
You: **Where** is your pen?
Your partner: My pen is **on** the desk.

WRITING: Describe Yourself

Write a paragraph about yourself.

Step 1. Read the information about the person below. Then complete the sentences.

Name: Engin Elmas
Age: 20
Job: Student
Nationality: Turkish

The man's name _____*is*_____ Engin Elmas. He
_____ 20 years old. He is a _____.
He _____ Turkish.

Step 2. Complete the information about yourself.

Name: _____

Age: _____

Job: _____

Nationality: _____

Step 3. Now write about yourself. Follow the model. For more writing guidelines, see pages 202-207.

My name is Engin Elmas. I am
20 years old...

A Choose the best answer, A, B, C, or D, to complete the sentence. Mark your answer by darkening the oval with the same letter.

1. Eggs _____ black.

    A. are not   Ⓐ Ⓑ Ⓒ Ⓓ
    B. isn't
    C. no are
    D. no is

2. A: Are you a student?
   B: Yes, _____.

    A. I'm   Ⓐ Ⓑ Ⓒ Ⓓ
    B. I am
    C. I'm not
    D. I'm student

3. _____ my grammar book?

    A. Is   Ⓐ Ⓑ Ⓒ Ⓓ
    B. When's
    C. Who's
    D. Where's

4. _____ the capital of Mexico?

    A. Who's   Ⓐ Ⓑ Ⓒ Ⓓ
    B. Is
    C. Where
    D. What's

5. The teacher is _____ the classroom.

    A. on   Ⓐ Ⓑ Ⓒ Ⓓ
    B. in
    C. at
    D. from

6. _____ are doctors.

    A. This woman   Ⓐ Ⓑ Ⓒ Ⓓ
    B. These woman
    C. These women
    D. These womans

7. They are _____.

    A. good childs   Ⓐ Ⓑ Ⓒ Ⓓ
    B. goods children
    C. good childrens
    D. good children

8. A: _____ that man?
   B: That's my father.

    A. Who   Ⓐ Ⓑ Ⓒ Ⓓ
    B. What's
    C. Who's
    D. What

9. _____ airplanes are big.

    A. Those   Ⓐ Ⓑ Ⓒ Ⓓ
    B. This
    C. They
    D. It

10. A: _____ at school today?
    B: Yes, he is.

    A. Is Ken   Ⓐ Ⓑ Ⓒ Ⓓ
    B. Ken
    C. Ken he is
    D. Ken is

B Find the underlined word or phrase, A, B, C, or D, that is incorrect. Mark your answer by darkening the oval with the same letter.

1. How old is the pyramids in Egypt?
   A   B   C   D

   Ⓐ Ⓑ Ⓒ Ⓓ

2. What are the name of the
   A   B   C

   seven continents?
   D

   Ⓐ Ⓑ Ⓒ Ⓓ

3. My brother is a student in an university
   A   B   C   D

   in my country.

   Ⓐ Ⓑ Ⓒ Ⓓ

4. Watches from Switzerland are expensives.
   A   B   C   D

   Ⓐ Ⓑ Ⓒ Ⓓ

5. That's my teacher in front the classroom.
   A   B   C   D

   Ⓐ Ⓑ Ⓒ Ⓓ

6. They're visitor from Guatemala in Central
   A   B   C   D

   America.

   Ⓐ Ⓑ Ⓒ Ⓓ

7. Good doctors are important in
   A   B   C

   an hospital.
   D

   Ⓐ Ⓑ Ⓒ Ⓓ

8. An horse is an intelligent animal.
   A   B   C   D

   Ⓐ Ⓑ Ⓒ Ⓓ

9. That man are a famous actor
            A   B   C

   in my country.
   D

   Ⓐ Ⓑ Ⓒ Ⓓ

10. Puerto Rico is a island and a country
                A   B   C

    in the Atlantic Ocean.
    D

    Ⓐ Ⓑ Ⓒ Ⓓ

UNIT 2

BE: IT, THERE, AND THE PAST TENSE OF BE

2a *It* to Talk about the Weather

It's hot.
It's sunny.
It's 90 degrees Fahrenheit/32 degrees centigrade.
Cindy is in the swimming pool.

We use *it* to talk about the weather.

   It's sunny.

Questions	Answers
	It's sunny.
How's the weather in Los Angeles?	**It**'s hot/cold.
	It's rainy.
What's the weather like today?	**It**'s windy.
	It's not cold.
What's the temperature today?	**It**'s 90 degrees Fahrenheit/32 degrees centigrade.

1 Practice

Write the answers to the questions about the weather map.

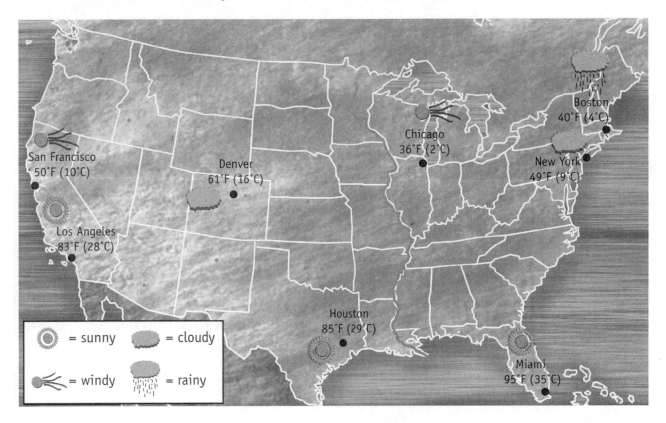

San Francisco
50°F (10°C)

Los Angeles
83°F (28°C)

Denver
61°F (16°C)

Chicago
36°F (2°C)

Boston
40°F (4°C)

New York
49°F (9°C)

Houston
85°F (29°C)

Miami
95°F (35°C)

= sunny   = cloudy

= windy   = rainy

1. What's the weather like in New York City? _It's cloudy_____.

2. Is it cold in New York today? _____.

3. What's the temperature in New York? _____.

4. What's the weather like in Houston? _____.

5. What's the temperature in Houston? _____.

6. What's the weather like in Los Angeles? _____.

7. What's the temperature in Los Angeles? _____.

8. Is it hot or cold in Chicago today? _____.

9. Is it sunny in Miami? _____.

10. What's the temperature in Miami? _____.

11. Is it windy in Boston? _____.

12. What's the weather like in Boston? _____.

13. How's the weather in San Francisco? _____.

14. Is it windy in Denver? _____.

15. How's the weather in Denver? _____.

16. What's the temperature in Denver? _____.

Be: It, There, and the Past Tense of *Be*

Practice

Work with a partner. Ask your partner about the weather today.

Example:
You: What's the weather like today?
Your partner: It's cool and cloudy.

2b *It* to Tell Time

Form / Function

What time is it?

It's eleven past 10:00.

1. We use **it** to talk about time, including days, dates, months, and years. (See pages 377 to 378 for days, months, and numbers.)

TIME		DAYS, DATES, MONTHS, YEARS	
Question	Answer	Questions	Answers
	It's two.	What day is **it**?	**It**'s Wednesday.
What time is **it**?	It's two o'clock.	What month is **it**?	**It**'s July.
		What year is **it**?	**It**'s 2002.
	It's two P.M.*	What's the date today?	**It**'s July 6th.

2. We can express the time in different ways.

      2:15   It's two fifteen.   OR   It's a quarter past two.
    10:35   It's ten thirty-five. OR   It's twenty-five to eleven.

3. When we say 12 A.M., it's midnight.

4. When we say 12 P.M., it's noon or midday.

    * A.M. = morning (before noon)
    * P.M. = after noon (between noon and midnight)

3 Practice

Say these times.

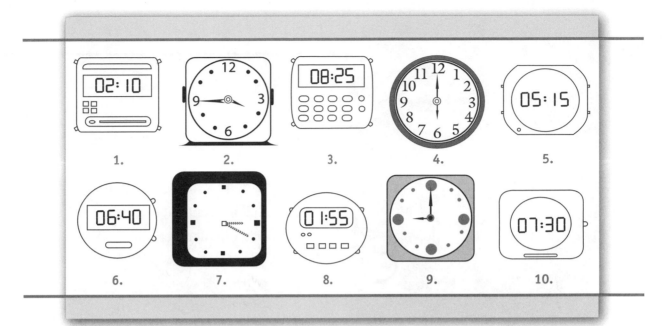

1. 2. 3. 4. 5.

6. 7. 8. 9. 10.

4 Practice

Match the question with the answer.

_e_	**1.** What time is it?	**a.** It's Monday.
____	**2.** What month is it?	**b.** It's 2003.
____	**3.** What year is it?	**c.** It's September.
____	**4.** What day is it?	**d.** It's September 10th.
____	**5.** What's the date today?	**e.** It's 2:30.

5 Practice

Work with a partner. Ask and answer questions.

1. What time is it?   **4.** What's the time?
2. What's the date today?   **5.** What year is it?
3. What month is it?   **6.** What day is it?

Be: It, There, and the Past Tense of *Be*

2c Questions with *When, What Day,* and *What Time;* Prepositions of Time

Form

When is Timmy's birthday?
It's **on** September 10th.
It's **on** Sunday.

WHEN

QUESTION			ANSWERS
When	Verb		
When	is	your birthday?	It's on September 10th*.
			On September 10th.
			September 10th.

WHAT

QUESTIONS				ANSWERS
What	Noun	Verb	Object	
What	**day**			It's on Sunday.
				On Sunday.
		is	the party?	
What	**time**			It's at 8:00.
				At 8:00.
				8:00.

* See ordinal numbers on page 197-198.

1. We use *when* or *what* for questions about time.

       When is your birthday?   It's on Sunday.

       What day is the party?   It's on Sunday.

       What time is the party?   It's at 8:00.

2. When we talk about time, we usually use the prepositions *in, on,* or *at.*

   a. We use *in* for parts of the day and with months, seasons, and years:

       in the morning, **in** the afternoon, **in** the evening

       in July, **in** August, **in** September

       in the spring, **in** the summer, **in** the autumn, **in** the winter

       in 1786, **in** 1942, **in** 2003

   b. We use *at* with *night*: **at** night

   c. We use *on* with days and dates:

       on Monday, **on** Tuesday morning

       on September 12th OR **on** the 12th of September

   d. We use *at* for times of the day:

       at 2 o'clock, **at** 5:15

3. We use *from...to* for the start and finish of something:

       from 9 **to** 10, **from** 7:30 **to** 11:15

---

6   Practice

Complete the sentences with the prepositions of time *in, on,* or *at.*

  1. I was born _____*in*_____ August.

  2. I was born _____ 1985.

  3. I was born _____ August 20, 1985.

  4. I get up _____ 7 o'clock.

  5. My class is _____ 9:15.

  6. I have class _____ Monday and Wednesday.

  7. I have class _____ the morning.

  8. I work _____ Tuesday and Thursday.

  9. I have class _____ the evening.

10. I study _____ night.

11. I go to bed _____ 11:30.

12. I have an appointment with my doctor _____ September 15th.

13. The appointment is _____the morning.

14. It's _____ 10:30.

Practice

Work with a partner. Ask and answer these questions about holidays. Then write the answers.

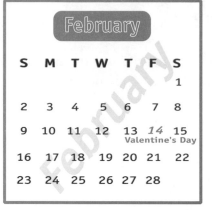
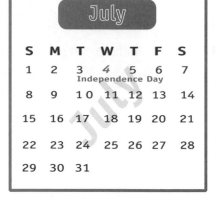

1. When is New Year's Day?   *It's on January 1ˢᵗ* _____.

2. What day is New Year's Day?   *It's on Wednesday* _____.

3. When is Christmas?   _____.

4. What day is Christmas?   _____.

5. When is Valentine's Day?   _____.

6. What day is Valentine's Day?   _____.

7. When is Independence Day?   _____.

8. What day is Independence Day?   _____.

9. When is Halloween?   _____.

10. What day is Halloween?   _____.

11. When is Thanksgiving?   _____.

12. What day is Thanksgiving?   _____.

8 Practice

Work with a partner. Ask and answer questions using phrases from the list.

Example:
You: When is the last day of class?
Your partner: It's on December 17th.

1. the last day of class
2. Christmas Day
3. the next test
4. the next school holiday
5. your birthday
6. Valentine's day

2d Statements with *There + Be*

Form

There is a table.
There are two cups on the table.
There isn't a glass of water.
There aren't four hands.

AFFIRMATIVE				
	There	*Be*	Subject	Location
Singular	**There**	**is**	a woman	at the table.
Plural	**There**	**are**	two cups	on the table.

NEGATIVE				
	There	*Be + Not*	Subject	Location
Singular	There	**isn't**	a glass	on the table.
Plural	There	**aren't**	any*glasses	on the table.

Contractions	
there is	there's
there is not	there isn't
	there's not
there are not	there aren't

* We use *any* before plural nouns that follow negative verbs and in yes/no questions.

Are there **any** cookies on the table? (yes/no question)
No, there aren't **any** cookies on the table. (negative verb)

41

Be: It, There, and the Past Tense of Be

1. We use *there is/there's* or *there are* to say something exists.

> **There's** a computer in the room.
> **There are** books on the desk.

2. We say *there isn't/there aren't* to say something doesn't exist.

> **There isn't** a waiter in the picture.
> **There aren't** any glasses on the table.

9 Practice

Look at Ted's kitchen. Complete the sentences with *there is* or *there are*.

1. *There is* _____ a table in the kitchen.
2. _____ two chairs.
3. _____ plates on the table.
4. _____ pots on the table.
5. _____ cups on the floor.
6. _____ a telephone on the floor.
7. _____ a pot on the stove.
8. _____ pots and dishes in the sink.
9. _____ a backpack under the table.
10. _____ a jacket on the chair.

10 Practice

Look at the photo and complete the sentences with *there's/there are* or *there isn't/there aren't.*

1. _There's_____ a woman at the desk.
2. _____ a desk.
3. _____ a laptop.
4. _____ a telephone.
5. _____ flowers.
6. _____ any books.
7. _____ a clock.
8. _____ papers.
9. _____ pens.
10. _____ any bottles of water.

11 Practice

Write ten sentences about things that are and are not in your classroom.

Things in the classroom

1. _There are desks_____.
2. _____.
3. _____.
4. _____.
5. _____.

Things not in the classroom

6. _There aren't any computers_____.
7. _____.
8. _____.
9. _____.
10. _____.

2e Questions with *There + Be*

Is there a big hotel near the lake?
No, **there isn't**.

QUESTIONS WITH *IS THERE/ARE THERE*				SHORT ANSWERS	
Be	*There*	Subject	Location	Affirmative	Negative
				Yes,	**No,**
Is	**there**	a bank	in the town?	there **is.**	there **isn't.**
Are	**there**	any shops		there **are.**	there **aren't.**

QUESTIONS WITH *HOW MANY*		
How Many	Plural Noun	*Be + There*
How many	restaurants	**are there**?

Practice

Read the brochure for a hotel resort. Then complete the questions and answers with *there is*, *there isn't*, *there are*, *there aren't*, *is there*, or *are there*. Use *how many* when necessary. Use *yes* and *no* as necessary.

Blue Lake Hotel

Welcome to the Blue Lake Hotel!

This is the view from the hotel. You are in the mountains in just five minutes.

There are 250 rooms in the hotel. There are three restaurants and over twenty shops. There is an exercise center, and there are two swimming pools.

There is an underground parking lot. There is also a train near the hotel. The train takes you to the town of Gertan in twenty minutes.

Come and relax in the mountains.

1. Is there a view from the hotel?

Yes, there is_____.

2. _____ mountains near the hotel?

Yes, _____.

3. _____ an exercise center?

_____.

4. _____ a bus service to the town?

No, _____.

45

Be: It, There, and the Past Tense of Be

5. _____ an underground parking lot?

_____.

6. _____ schools near the hotel?

No, _____.

7. How many rooms are there in the hotel?

_____.

8. _____ a movie theater?

No, _____.

9. _____ a train near the hotel?

_____.

10. How many swimming pools _____?

_____.

11. How many restaurants _____?

_____.

12. _____ shops _____?

_____.

13 Practice

Write questions with *how many* using the prompts. Then write answers to the questions.

1. minutes/an hour   _How many minutes are there in an hour_____?

_There are 60_____._

2. hours/a day   _____?

_____.

3. days/a week   _____?

_____.

4. days/a year   _____?

_____.

5. weeks/a year _____?

_____.

6. hours/a week _____?

_____.

7. centimeters/a meter _____?

_____.

8. inches/a foot _____?

_____.

14 Practice

Work with a partner or a group. Think of a word. Your partner or the group has to find the word. Ask and answer questions with *is there, are there, there is,* or *there are.*

Example:

Question: How many letters are there in the word?

Answer: There are eight letters.

Question: Is there an *e* in it?

Answer: Yes, there is.

(Continue until someone finds the word.)

15 Your Turn

Work in pairs or groups. Use *it* and *there* + *be* to ask and answer questions about your hometowns. The following topics may help you.

beach	parks	shopping malls	tourists
mountains	river	subway	

Example:

1. What's the weather like in the summer?   It's very hot.

2. Is it rainy in the winter?   Yes, it is.

3. Is there a beach near your hometown?   No, there isn't.

4. Are there parks in your hometown?   Yes, there are.

Be: It, There, and the Past Tense of Be

2f The Conjunctions *And, But,* and *Or*

John is working, **but** he is not in the office.

1. We use a comma before the conjunctions *and, but,* and *or* when we connect two sentences.

   The food at this restaurant is delicious, **and** it's cheap.
   The food is cheap, **but** it's not good.
   We can go to an Italian restaurant, **or** we can go to a Chinese restaurant.

2. We do not use a comma when the conjunction separates two descriptive adjectives.

   The food is good **and** cheap.
   She is tired **but** happy.
   It's good **or** bad.

3. We do not use a comma when the conjunction separates two nouns or prepositional phrases.

   There are closets **and** windows in my apartment.
   Are you busy Saturday **or** Sunday?
   There are oranges in the refrigerator **and** on the table.

Function

We use *and, but,* and *or* to join two sentences.

Conjunction	Function	Example
and	Adds information.	The coat is beautiful. It is warm. The coat is beautiful, **and** it is warm.
but	Gives a contrasting idea.	I want to go skiing. I don't have the money. I want to go skiing, **but** I don't have the money.
or	Gives a choice.	We go. We stay. We go, **or** we stay.

16

Practice

Complete the sentences with *and, but,* or *or*.

1. Our school is old, _____*but*_____ it is clean.
2. The classrooms are sunny _____ bright.
3. There are old tables _____ chairs in our classroom.
4. The chairs are old, _____ they are strong.
5. There are two cafeterias. There is a cafeteria for the students, _____ there is a cafeteria for the teachers.
6. We sell two kinds of food: hot food like pizza _____ cold food like sandwiches.
7. Is your English class in the morning _____ in the afternoon?
8. In my class, there are students from Mexico, _____ there are students from Japan.
9. Are there 18 _____ 19 students in our class?
10. Is your teacher funny _____ serious?
11. My English class is great, _____ I have a lot of homework.
12. Is your book blue, _____ is it green?

17 Practice

Join the ideas in A and B. Then write sentences with *and, but,* and *or*. Use commas correctly.

A	B
_c_ **1.** He's not rich	**a.** it's warm today.
_____ **2.** It's winter	**b.** afternoon?
_____ **3.** What's the best time for you? Morning	**c.** he has an expensive car.
_____ **4.** It's late	**d.** Italian.
_____ **5.** Is a tomato a fruit	**e.** bad?
_____ **6.** Is this milk good	**f.** a vegetable?
_____ **7.** She speaks Spanish, French,	**g.** the food is very good.
_____ **8.** The restaurant is clean	**h.** I'm tired. Let's go home.

1. *He's not rich, but he has an expensive car* .

2. _____ .

3. _____ .

4. _____ .

5. _____ .

6. _____ .

7. _____ .

8. _____ .

18 Your Turn

A. Write four things about where you live.

Example:
There are two bedrooms in my apartment.

1. _____ .

2. _____ .

3. _____ .

4. _____ .

B. Read your partner's sentences. Now write four sentences about your home and your partner's home.

Example:
My apartment has two bedrooms, but Tom's apartment has one bedroom.

1. _____

   _____ .

2. _____

   _____ .

3. _____

   _____ .

4. _____

   _____ .

2g The Past Tense of *Be*: Affirmative and Negative Statements

Bertie and
Brenda today

Bertie and Brenda
50 years ago

Bertie and Brenda **are** happy today.

They **were** happy 50 years ago.

Brenda **was** 25 years old in the photo.

Bertie **was** 30 years old in the photo.

Subject	Be (Not)			Time Expression
I	was (not)			yesterday.
You	were (not)			two hours ago.
He/She/It	was (not)	here		three weeks ago.
We	were (not)			four months ago.
They				last night/week/month/year.
				in 1980.

Contractions	
was not	wasn't
were not	weren't

We use *was* and *were* to talk about the past. For this reason, we often use time expressions like *yesterday, four hours ago, last week, twenty years ago,* and *in 1995* with *was* and *were.*

> It **was** cold **yesterday**.
> We **weren't** in New York **in 1998**.

19 Practice

Complete the sentences with *is, was, are,* **or** *were.*

1. Today Bertie _____*is*_____ 80 years old.
2. Fifty years ago, Bertie _____ an engineer.
3. Brenda _____ a secretary 50 years ago.
4. Brenda _____ 75 years old today.
5. Bertie and Brenda _____ out most of the time 50 years ago.
6. Fifty years ago, they _____ in the city most of the time.
7. Today they _____ on their farm.
8. They _____ with their grandchildren today.
9. Bertie and Brenda _____ happy 50 years ago.
10. Bertie and Brenda _____ happy today.

20 Practice

Complete the sentences with *wasn't* **or** *weren't.*

1. Gina was with her friends and family yesterday. She _____*wasn't*_____ alone.
2. Gina was in a white dress yesterday. She _____ in her office clothes.
3. It was a special day for Gina. It _____ a regular day.
4. Gina was in a special building yesterday. She _____ in the office.
5. Her friends and family were very happy yesterday. They _____ sad.
6. Her friends were with her. They _____ at work.

21 What Do You Think?

What happened in Gina's life yesterday?

22 Practice

Complete the sentences about Leonardo da Vinci and Michelangelo with *was, were, wasn't,* or *weren't.*

Michelangelo
Italian
painter
young (when in Florence)
architect
single

Leonardo da Vinci
Italian
painter
old (when in Florence)
architect
inventor & engineer
single

Leonardo da Vinci and Michelangelo _____*were*_____ Italians. Both Leonardo da Vinci
                                              1

and Michelangelo _____ famous painters. They _____ both in Florence,
                        2   3

Italy at the same time. Leonardo _____ young, but Michelangelo _____
                                       4   5

young. Leonardo and Michelangelo _____ architects too. Leonardo
                                         6

_____ an inventor, but Michelangelo _____ an inventor. Leonardo
      7   8

_____ an engineer, but Michelangelo _____ an engineer. Leonardo
      9   10

_____ single, and Michelangelo _____ single. Both Leonardo and
      11   12

Michelangelo _____ not married.
                   13

The Past Tense of *Be*: Questions

Johnny: **Was** Mozart a musician?

Amy: Yes, he **was.**

Johnny: **Was** he German?

Amy: No, he **wasn't.**

Johnny: What nationality **was** he?

Amy: He **was** Austrian.

Johnny: Oh.

YES/NO QUESTIONS				SHORT ANSWERS	
Be	Subject		Time Expression	Affirmative	Negative
				Yes,	**No,**
Was	I			you **were.**	you **weren't.**
Were	you			I **was.**	I **wasn't.**
Was	he/she/it	here	yesterday?	he/she/it **was.**	he/she/it **wasn't.**
	we			you **were.**	you **weren't.**
Were	you			we **were.**	we **weren't.**
	they			they **were.**	they **weren't.**

WH- QUESTIONS				ANSWERS
Wh- Word	*Be*	Subject		
Where	**were**	you	born?	I **was** born in Tokyo.
When	**was**	I	there?	You **were** there 3 years ago.
What	**was**	she?		She **was** an actress.
How old	**were**	they?		They **were** nineteen.

23 Practice

Work with a partner. Write questions about a new restaurant using the prompts. Then ask and answer the questions.

1. the food/good   *Was the food good* _____?
2. the food/expensive   _____?
3. the servers/polite   _____?
4. the restaurant/clean _____?
5. the place/busy   _____?
6. the restaurant/easy to get to _____?
7. the plates/full   _____?
8. the service/good   _____?
9. the restaurant/big   _____?
10. the food/tasty   _____?
11. the menu/Italian   _____?

24 Practice

Work with a partner. Ask and answer questions about famous people from the past. Write the questions and answers on the lines.

1. Napoleon/a musician   *Was Napoleon a musician* _____?
   No, he wasn't _____.

2. Mozart/a painter   _____?
   _____

3. Marilyn Monroe/Chinese _____?
   _____.

4. George Washington and John F. Kennedy/presidents of the United States
   _____?
   _____.

5. The Beatles/French   _____?
   _____.

6. Princess Diana/American _____?
   _____.

7. Cleopatra/Egyptian   _____?
   _____.

Be: It, There, and the Past Tense of Be

8. Picasso/politician

_____ ?

_____ .

9. Mozart and Beethoven/musicians

_____ ?

_____ .

10. Elvis Presley/a singer

_____ ?

_____ .

25 Practice

Work with a partner. Think of a famous person from history. Ask yes/no questions with _be_ **to find out who the person was.**

Example:
You: Was he a man or a woman?
Your partner: He was a man.
You: Was he American?
Your partner: Yes, he was.

26 Practice

Match the questions and answers.

QUESTIONS

  _c_ **1.** When were your grandparents married?

_____ **2.** How old was your grandfather?

_____ **3.** What was your grandfather?

_____ **4.** How old was your grandmother?

_____ **5.** Where was the wedding?

_____ **6.** Was it a big wedding?

ANSWERS

a. He was a bank manager.

b. It was in Boston.

c. In 1932.

d. He was 30 years old.

e. Yes, it was.

f. She was 22.

27 Your Turn

Answer the six questions in Practice 26 about your own grandparents or other people you know. Then add four more sentences about them.

Example:
My grandparents were married in 1954.

1. _____.
2. _____.
3. _____.
4. _____.
5. _____.
6. _____.
7. _____.
8. _____.
9. _____.
10. _____.

28 Your Turn

Ask your partner questions about his/her birthday. Use *where*, *when*, and *how*.

Examples:
1. Where were you born?

2. When was your last birthday?

3. Where were you on your birthday?

4. How old were you?

WRITING: Describe a Place

Write a postcard about your vacation.

Step 1. Work with a partner. You are on vacation. Ask and answer questions about your hotel using the prompts.

Example:

name

You: What's the name of the hotel?
Your partner: The name of the hotel is Paradise Hotel.

what	the weather	swimming pool	restaurant
how old	stores	many tourists	gym
your room	a view	name	is there/are there

Step 2. Write the answers to the questions from Step 1.

Step 3. Read this postcard.

Dear Lin,

I am at the Palace Hotel on the beach in Hawaii. It is sunny and hot today. The temperature is about 90 degrees, but it's nice. The hotel is wonderful. There is a swimming pool, and there is a gym. There are restaurants and stores in the hotel. There are tourists from many countries. The view from my hotel room is wonderful. I love it here.

Love,

Julie

Step 4. Write a postcard like the one above, but use your answers from Step 2. For more writing guidelines, see pages 202-207.

Step 5. Work with a partner to edit your postcard. Check spelling, punctuation, vocabulary, and grammar.

Step 6. Write your final postcard.

SELF-TEST

A   **Choose the best answer, A, B, C, or D, to complete the sentence. A dash (–) means that no word is needed to complete the sentence. Mark your answer by darkening the oval with the same letter.**

1. How many states _____ in the United States?

    A. there is   Ⓐ Ⓑ Ⓒ Ⓓ
    B. is there
    C. are there
    D. there are

2. _____ any mountains in Mexico?

    A. There is   Ⓐ Ⓑ Ⓒ Ⓓ
    B. Is there
    C. Are there
    D. There are

3. Thomas Edison was born _____ 1847.

    A. on   Ⓐ Ⓑ Ⓒ Ⓓ
    B. in
    C. at
    D. by

4. _____ cold at the South Pole.

    A. It is   Ⓐ Ⓑ Ⓒ Ⓓ
    B. There is
    C. Is it
    D. It has

5. Is a tomato a fruit, _____ is it a vegetable?

    A. and   Ⓐ Ⓑ Ⓒ Ⓓ
    B. but
    C. or
    D. there

6. _____ 30 million people in Tokyo, Japan.

    A. Are there   Ⓐ Ⓑ Ⓒ Ⓓ
    B. There are
    C. It is
    D. There is

7. The airport is open _____ night.

    A. in   Ⓐ Ⓑ Ⓒ Ⓓ
    B. —
    C. on
    D. at

8. Princess Diana died _____ August 1997.

    A. in   Ⓐ Ⓑ Ⓒ Ⓓ
    B. at
    C. on
    D. from

9. Princess Diana died _____ August 31, 1997.

    A. in   Ⓐ Ⓑ Ⓒ Ⓓ
    B. at
    C. on
    D. —

10. Days are short _____ winter.

    A. at   Ⓐ Ⓑ Ⓒ Ⓓ
    B. in
    C. on
    D. the

Be: It, There, and the Past Tense of *Be*

B **Find the underlined word or phrase, A, B, C, or D, that is incorrect. Mark your answer by darkening the oval with the same letter.**

1. There is nine-fifteen in Los Angeles but
   A   B

   it is six-fifteen in New York.
   C   D

   Ⓐ Ⓑ Ⓒ Ⓓ

2. Canada but the United States are in
   A   B   C D

   North America.

   Ⓐ Ⓑ Ⓒ Ⓓ

3. Marie Curie is a French scientist, but she
   A   B

   was born in Poland in 1859.
   C   D

   Ⓐ Ⓑ Ⓒ Ⓓ

4. The Chinese New Year is on January or
   A   B C   D

   February.

   Ⓐ Ⓑ Ⓒ Ⓓ

5. It is winter in Canada, or it is summer
   A   B   C

   in Argentina.
   D

   Ⓐ Ⓑ Ⓒ Ⓓ

6. Valentine's Day is in February 14, but
   A   B

   it is not a holiday.
   C   D

   Ⓐ Ⓑ Ⓒ Ⓓ

7. There aren't any trees in Antarctica
   A   B   C

   because there is very cold there.
           D

   Ⓐ Ⓑ Ⓒ Ⓓ

8. Thanksgiving Day in the United States is
   A   B   C

   always in Thursday.
          D

   Ⓐ Ⓑ Ⓒ Ⓓ

9. There is one hundred centimeters in one
   A B   C   D

   meter.

   Ⓐ Ⓑ Ⓒ Ⓓ

10. George Washington and John F. Kennedy
                       A

    was American presidents.
    B   C   D

    Ⓐ Ⓑ Ⓒ Ⓓ

UNIT 3

THE SIMPLE PRESENT TENSE

3a The Simple Present Tense

Janet **works** in an office.
She **sits** at her desk and **types** on a computer.

Subject	Verb	Subject	Verb
I			
You	work.	He	
We		She	works.
They		It	

The verb after *he, she,* or *it* takes a final *-s.*

Function

She **speaks** on the telephone
and **types** on her computer.

We use the simple present tense when we talk about what people do all the time, or again and again.

1   Practice

Read the sentences about a typical day for Janet. Underline the correct form of the verb.

1. The alarm clock (ring/<u>rings</u>) at 7:00 every morning.

2. Janet (turn/turns) off the alarm clock.

3. She (get/gets) up.

4. She (walk/walks) to the bathroom.

5. She (take/takes) a shower.

6. She (comb/combs) her hair.

7. Janet says, "I (brush/brushes) my teeth every morning."

8. She (put/puts) on her clothes.

9. Janet (eat/eats) breakfast with her sister Meg.

10. They (drink/drinks) coffee.

11. They (eat/eats) cereal.

12. They (watch/watches) the news on television.

13. Meg (stay/stays) home.

14. They (say/says) goodbye.

15. Janet (lock/locks) the door.

16. She (wait/waits) for the bus.

17. She (get/gets) on a bus.

18. She (pay/pays) the bus driver.

19. She (sit/sits) down on a seat.

20. She (get/gets) off the bus at the same place every day.

---

2 Your Turn

A. Write five things you do every day.

1. _I get up at 7:30_____.

2. _____.

3. _____.

4. _____.

5. _____.

B. Write five things a friend does every day.

1. _____.

2. _____.

3. _____.

4. _____.

5. _____.

3b Adverbs of Frequency

Penguins **never** fly.

Penguins **usually** eat fish.

Penguins **often** swim.

Always, usually, often, sometimes, rarely, and *never* are adverbs of frequency. We often use them with simple present tense verbs. They come between the subject and the verb.

Subject	Adverb of Frequency	Simple Present Tense	
I	**always**	do	my homework.
You	**usually**	get up	early.
Tony	**often**	listens	to the radio.
She	**sometimes**	drinks	tea.
We	**rarely**	go	to the theater.
Penguins	**never**	fly.	

Function

Brenda **always** walks home from school.

Adverbs of frequency tell us how many times something happens.

		Mon.	Tues.	Wed.	Thurs.	Fri.	Sat.	Sun.
I **always** walk in the morning.	100%							
Julia **usually** walks in the morning.								
We **often** walk in the morning.								
You **sometimes** walk in the morning.								
Mel and Sue **rarely** walk in the morning.								
Satoshi **never** walks in the morning.	0%							

3 Practice

Add the adverb of frequency on the left to each sentence.

1. I get up at 7:00.

always *I always get up at 7:00* .

2. I have breakfast at 7:30.

usually _____.

3. I drink two cups of tea for breakfast.

often _____.

4. I eat eggs for breakfast.

never _____.

5. I watch the morning news on television.

sometimes _____.

6. I listen to the radio at home.

rarely _____.

7. I read the newspaper in the morning.

usually _____.

8. I lock my door.

always _____.

9. I take the bus to work.

usually _____.

10. I take a taxi.

rarely _____.

11. I get to work on time.

often _____.

12. I arrive late.

sometimes _____.

4 Your Turn

What do you do on weekday evenings? Use *always, usually, often, sometimes,* *rarely,* **or** *never* **with the following phrases or your own.**

Example:

I rarely go to the movies on weekday evenings.

1. eat dinner early
2. watch TV
3. go to bed late
4. read magazines
5. see friends

6. speak English
7. go to the movies
8. do homework
9. stay at home
10. drink tea after dinner

3c Adverbs of Frequency with *Be*

Form

Yukio is **always** on time.
Yukio is **never** late.
He **always** catches his train at 7:00.
Yukio is late today. He is very upset.

1. We put adverbs of frequency after the verb *be*.

Subject	Simple Present Tense of *Be*	Adverb of Frequency	
Ted	is	always usually often sometimes rarely never	late.

2. We put adverbs of frequency before all other verbs.

Subject	Adverb of Frequency	Simple Present Tense Verb	
Ted	sometimes	comes	late.

5 Practice

Add the adverb of frequency on the left to each sentence.

1. always   Yukio is on time.   <u>Yukio is always on time</u>.

2. always   Yukio comes to work on time. _____.

3. never   Yukio is sick. _____.

4. usually   He works on Saturday. _____.

5. sometimes   He is at work on Sundays. _____.

6. sometimes   He feels tired. _____.

7. rarely   He is home early. _____.

8. often   He works late at the office. _____.

9. rarely   He takes a vacation. _____.

10. never   He misses a meeting. _____.

11. usually   He is in his office. _____.

12. rarely   He is late with his work. _____.

13. often   He goes to bed late. _____.

14. often   He is at his desk at lunch. _____.

15. rarely   He has time for his family. _____.

6 Your Turn

Write six things about what you do every day with *always, usually, often, sometimes, rarely,* and *never*. Use the following phrases or your own.

get up   drink tea   exercise   early/late to school   do homework   go to bed

1. <u>I always go to bed late</u>.
2. _____.
3. _____.
4. _____.
5. _____.
6. _____.

3d Spelling and Pronunciation of Final –s and –es

Form

Every evening, Len **sits** in front of the television, **drinks** his coffee, **watches** his favorite program, and **falls** asleep.

Verb	Spelling	Examples	Pronunciation
Verb ends in voiceless f, k, p, t. **like work sleep**	Add –s.	He like**s** coffee. He work**s**. It sleep**s**.	/s/
Verb ends in voiced b, d, g, l, m, n, r, v or vowel. **swim read run**	Add –s.	He swim**s**. She read**s**. He run**s**.	/z/
Verb ends in ch, sh, s, x, z.* **watch dress finish**	Add –es.	She watch**es** TV. He dress**es**. It finish**es** at 10:00.	/iz/
Verb ends in consonant + y. **worry cry hurry**	Drop y, add -ies.	He worr**ies** a lot. The baby cr**ies** at night. She hurr**ies** to work.	/z/
Verb ends in vowel + y. **play stay buy**	Add –s.	He play**s** football. She stay**s** at home. He buy**s** food.	/z/

*Verbs that end in *dge,* as in **judge,** add only –s but are pronounced with /iz/ at the end.

7 Practice

Write the third person singular of the following verbs in the correct column, and then read them out loud.

ask	dance	kiss	pass	see	try
begin	drink	like	play	speak	walk
brush	eat	look	put	stay	wash
buy	fix	miss	rain	stop	wish
catch	fly	open	say	teach	write

/s/	/iz/	/z/
puts	brushes	says
_____	_____	_____
_____	_____	_____
_____	_____	_____
_____	_____	_____
_____	_____	_____
_____	_____	_____
_____	_____	_____
_____	_____	_____
_____	_____	_____

8 Practice

Complete the sentences with the third person singular of the verb in parentheses. Then circle the correct pronunciation for each verb.

Dan Thomas (come) _____comes_____ (s /ⓩ/ iz) from Canada but he (live)

_____ (s / z / iz) in New York. He (teach) _____ (s / z / iz) English.
　　　2　　　　　　　　　　　　　　　　　　　　　　　　　　　3

He (like) _____ (s / z / iz) to walk, so he (walk) _____ (s / z / iz)
　　　　　4　　　　　　　　　　　　　　　　　　　　　　　　　　　　5

to school every day. He always (arrive) _____ (s / z / iz)in class on time. He
　　　　　　　　　　　　　　　　　　　　　6

(enjoy) _____ (s / z / iz) his job and (love) _____ (s / z / iz)
　　　　　7　　　　　　　　　　　　　　　　　　　　　　　　　　　8

his students. He never (miss) _____ (s / z / iz) a class. He usually (give)
　　　　　　　　　　　　　　　　9

_____ (s / z / iz) a lot of homework and (ask) _____ (s / z / iz)
　　　10　　　　　　　　　　　　　　　　　　　　　　　　　　　11

a lot of questions in class. He always (correct) _____ (s / z / iz) the home-
　　　　　　　　　　　　　　　　　　　　　　12

work and (give) _____ (s / z / iz) the homework back the next day. He
　　　　　　　　13

(speak) _____ (s / z / iz) English fast and always (forget) _____
　　　　　14　　　　　　　　　　　　　　　　　　　　　　　　　　　　　　15

(s/z/iz) the names of the students. He always (finish) _____ (s / z / iz) the
　　　　　　　　　　　　　　　　　　　　　　　　　16

class late.

9 What Do You Think?

Is Dan Thomas a good or bad teacher? Why?

10 Practice

Complete the sentences about Wendy with the words on the left.

1. try, always	Wendy _____*always tries*_____ hard.	
2. study, usually	She _____ in the library after class.	
3. worry, often	She _____ about her homework and her tests.	
4. stay, never	She _____ out with her friends after school.	
5. play, rarely	She _____ sports or games.	
6. enjoy, rarely	She _____ her life.	
7. be, often	She _____ unhappy.	
8. cry, sometimes	She _____.	
9. say, usually	She _____ she is happy and fine.	
10. look, often	But she _____ sad.	

3e Irregular Verbs: *Have, Do,* and *Go*

Kathy's classes finish at 4:00 every day.
Then she **goes** home.
She **has** a cup of coffee and **does** her homework.

The third person forms of *have, go,* and *do* are irregular.

I **have** a job.	He She **has** a problem. It
I **do** the work.	He She **does** the work. It
I **go** to work.	He She **goes** outside. It

11 Practice

Complete the sentences about Kathy and Kay with the verbs in parentheses.

1. Both Kathy and Kay (go) ___*go*___ to work.

2. Kathy (go) _____ to work in a hospital.

3. Kay (go) _____ to work in a big office.

4. Both Kathy and Kay (have) _____ cars.

5. Kathy (have) _____ a big car.

6. Kay (have) _____ a small car.

7. Both Kathy and Kay (do) _____ yoga to be healthy.

8. Kathy (do) _____ yoga in a gym.

9. Kay (do) _____ yoga at home.

12 Practice

Complete the sentences with the words in parentheses. Use the simple present tense.

Mike (have) _____ *has* _____ two classes in the morning. At 12:00,
                          1

he (finish) _____ his classes and (go) _____
                    2   3

to the cafeteria. He (eat) _____ lunch with his classmates. After
                                    4

lunch, he (study, usually) _____ in the library. His teachers
                                    5

(give, often) _____ a lot of homework. Then, he
                      6

(take) _____ the bus to his uncle's garage.
              7

   He (enjoy) _____ his work at the garage. He
                        8

(fix) _____ cars and (talk) _____ to people.
            9   10

His uncle (pay) _____ him every week. The garage
                        11

(close) _____ at 8:00.
                12

   After work, Mike (walk) _____ home. The garage is near his
                                    13

apartment. Mike (have) _____ a roommate, Len. Len
                                14

(be) _____ very nice. He (try, always) _____ to
            15   16

help Mike. Len and Mike (cook) _____ dinner and then they
                                          17

(eat) _____ in the kitchen. They (talk, always) _____
              18   19

a lot. Len (do, always) _____ the dishes. They
                                20

(watch, usually) _____ television. They (like) _____
                          21   22

football and other sports on TV. They (go, often) _____ to bed late.
                                                              23

13 Your Turn

Say three things a person does in his or her job. Your partner or the class guesses the job.

Example:
You: He/she has long holidays. He/she works with young people.
              He/she gives homework.
Your partner: A teacher.

3f *Have* and *Has*

He **has the flu**.
He **has a temperature**.
He **has** a thermometer in his mouth.
He **has a headache** too.
He **has** an ice-pack on his head.

	Singular			Plural		
I You	**have**			We		
He She It	**has**	a book.		You They	**have**	books.

Function

We use *have* and *has*:

1. For things we possess or own.

    I **have** a car.   She **has** two houses.

2. To describe people, places, animals, and things.

    It **has** two windows.   She **has** black hair.

3. For our families and people we know.

    I **have** a son.   She **has** a friend from Canada.

4. With some expressions like the following.

have a cold/the flu	The children **have a cold** this week.
have a temperature	I **have a temperature**.
have a headache/toothache	Gloria **has a toothache**.
have a problem	We **have a problem**.

14 Practice

Complete the sentences with *have* or *has*.

Sam ____*has*____ a good job. He _____ a wife, Kate. They _____ two
                    1   2   3
children. Kate _____ a good job, too. She is a teacher. They _____ one car
                      4   5
and they _____ a small house. The house _____ two bedrooms. It
                 6   7
_____ a garden, too. The garden _____ trees and flowers. Sam and his
        8   9
family are happy. They _____ a good life.
                              10

15 Practice

Complete the sentence with *is* or *has*.

1. Sam ____*is*____ young.

2. He _____ 28 years old.

3. He _____ healthy.

4. Today Sam _____ a problem.

5. He _____ sick.

6. He _____ a cold.

7. He _____ a headache too.

8. Sam _____ at home today.

16 Your Turn

A. From the following list, tell your partner five things you have. Use the list for ideas.

apartment	car	house	problem
brother/sister	dictionary	job	

Example:
I have a sister.

B. Write five sentences that tell what your partner has.

Example:
She has a brother and a sister.

1. _____.

2. _____.

3. _____.

4. _____.

5. _____.

3g The Simple Present Tense: Negative

Len **doesn't walk** in the evenings.

Len **doesn't see** his friends.

Len **doesn't go** out.

Len watches television and eats chips.

1. In present tense negative statements, *do* and *does* are auxiliary verbs. The base verb does not take an *–s* for the third person singular. The *–s* ending is on the helping verb *(does)*.

Subject	*Do Not/Does Not*	Base Verb
I You We They	**do not** **don't**	**work.**
He She It	**does not** **doesn't**	

2. We usually use contractions when we speak. We often use contractions when we write.

Contractions	
do not	don't
does not	doesn't

17 **Practice**

Complete the negative sentence with the words on the left.

1. understand, not   I like my husband Len but I

       _____ *don't understand* _____ him.

2. want, not   He is always tired. He _____

       to go out.

3. talk, not   He watches TV all the time.

       He _____ to me.

4. go, not   We _____ to the movies.

5. eat, not   He eats only chips and pizza.

       He _____ salads.

6. drink, not   He always drinks coffee.

       He _____ water.

7. like, not   He likes to watch sports on TV.

       He _____ to exercise.

8. have, not   We _____ many friends.

9. call, not   His friends _____.

10. see, not   His mother _____ him.

11. speak, not   His daughter _____ to him.

12. know, not   Poor Len, I _____ what to do!

18 **Practice**

Write true sentences with these words. Make the sentences negative where necessary.

1. birds/give milk   *Birds don't give milk* _____ .

2. fish/swim   _____ .

3. a chicken/come from an egg   _____ .

4. plants/need/water to grow   _____ .

5. penguins/live/Italy   _____ .

6. elephants/eat/chickens   _____ .

7. rice/grow/on trees   _____.

8. The Chinese/drink/tea   _____.

9. rain/come from/the sky   _____.

10. lions/eat/meat   _____.

11. a chicken/give/milk   _____.

12. giraffes/live/in Africa   _____.

19   Practice

Complete the sentences with the negative of the verbs from the list.

be	get up	look at	sit	wait
eat	go	put on	talk	worry

It is August. The sun is hot. There _____*aren't*_____ any clouds in the sky.
                                                                     1

Tony is in Hawaii. He _____ early. He gets up at 11:00.
                                              2

He _____ his shirt and tie. He puts on his shorts.
                        3

He _____ to work. He goes to the beach. He _____
                        4   5

for the bus. He waits for his friends. Tony and his friends _____ in
                                                                            6

front of computers. They sit in front of a table in a café on the beach.

They _____ about work. They talk about fun things to do. They
                        7

_____ sandwiches. They eat delicious food.
                  8

They _____ computers. They look at the blue sea.
                        9

Tony _____ about his work. He is happy and relaxed. But Tony isn't on
                        10

vacation. He is in his office. It's just a dream.

20   Your Turn

Say six things you *do* and six things you *don't* do on the weekend. Use phrases from the list or your own.

get up early	study English	go to school	do homework	go to the store
clean your room	see friends	play sports	have breakfast	

Example:
I don't get up early. I get up late.

3h The Simple Present Tense: Yes/No Questions

Meg: **Does** John wear glasses?
Linda: Yes, he **does.**
Meg: **Does** he wear glasses all the time?
Linda: Yes, he **does.**

1. We use *do* or *does* to make questions in the simple present. We always use the base form after *do* or *does*.

2. We often use *do* or *does* in short answers to questions.

| YES/NO QUESTIONS | | | SHORT ANSWERS | |
Do/Does	Subject	Base Verb	Affirmative	Negative
			Yes,	**No,**
Do	I		you **do.**	you **don't.**
	you		I/we **do.**	I/we **don't.**
	we		you **do.**	you **don't.**
	they	**work?**	they **do.**	they **don't.**
Does	he		he **does.**	he **doesn't.**
	she		she **does.**	she **doesn't.**
	it		it **does.**	it **doesn't.**

21 Practice

Penny wants to marry Tim. Her mother asks her questions about him. Write questions with *do* or *does*. Give short answers.

1. you/love him   *Do you love him* ?
   Yes   *Yes, I do* .

2. you/know his family   _____?
   Yes   _____.

3. he/have a good job   _____?
   Yes   _____.

4. he/live in a nice apartment _____?
   Yes   _____.

5. he/drive a nice car   _____?

    Yes   _____.

6. he/wear nice clothes   _____?

    Yes   _____.

7. he/smoke   _____?

    No   _____.

8. he/buy you nice gifts   _____?

    Yes   _____.

9. he/take you out   _____?

    Yes   _____.

10. he/want to marry you   _____?

    No   _____.

22   Read

Read about Tony Ku. With a partner, ask ten questions with *is, do,* or *does*. Give short answers.

    This is Tony Ku. He is a student in New York City. Tony lives in New York City, but he comes from Singapore. His family lives in Singapore. He misses his family. His brother and sister come to visit him in New York every year. He is very happy when they are with him. He goes to school every day. He speaks English and wants to be an actor. In the evening, he works in a restaurant. He is a waiter. He is a very good waiter. People love him.

Example:
You: Is he a student in New York City?
Your partner: Yes, he is.

Your Turn

You are looking for a roommate. Ask your partner six questions with *be* or *do*. Use the following words or your own. Your partner gives short answers.

clean	go to bed late	like parties
cook	have many friends	smoke

Example:
You: Do you listen to loud music?
Your partner: No, I don't.

3i   The Simple Present Tense: Wh- Questions

Form / Function

Sue: **Where do** kangaroos **come** from?

Ken: Australia.

Sue: **What do** they **eat**?

Ken: Plants. (They eat plants.)

Sue: **When do** they **sleep**?

Ken: In the day. (They sleep in the daytime.)

1. We often call *where, when, what, why, who, how,* and *how many* wh- question words because most of them start with the letters *wh*. We use wh- question words to get information.

2. We put question words before *do* and *does*.

3. Frequency adverbs like *usually* come after the subject in a question.

    When do you **usually** get up?   I **usually** get up at seven.

Wh- Word	*Do/Does*	Subject	Base Verb
What	do	I	do?
Where	does	he	live?
When	do	they	sleep?
Why	do	you	get up early?
Who	does	she	call?
How many	do	they	have?
How	do	you	go?

Practice

This is Paul. He plays in a group called the Purrmaster 9000. Match the questions to the answers.

A		B
_e_	**1.** What instrument does he play?	**a.** Songs.
____	**2.** Who does he play with?	**b.** Because he plays in concerts in different towns.
____	**3.** Where does he live?	**c.** In a small bus.
____	**4.** What does he write?	**d.** His brothers.
____	**5.** Why does he travel a lot?	**e.** The guitar.
____	**6.** When does he work?	**f.** He has five.
____	**7.** How many guitars does he have?	**g.** In Los Angeles.
____	**8.** How does he travel?	**h.** In the evenings.

Read

Read about Linda Barton. Then write questions with the words provided and give answers.

Linda lives in Toronto. She is married to Tom. Tom is an accountant. They have a daughter, Nancy. She is 20 years old and goes to the university. Linda is a nurse. She works in a big hospital. She starts work at 9:30 in the evening and finishes at 8:00 in the morning. She comes home and has breakfast. After breakfast she usually watches television and then goes to bed at about 10:00. She gets up at 4:00 in the afternoon, goes to the store, and prepares dinner. Her husband comes home at 7:00. They eat dinner. After dinner they talk. They also watch television together. Then at 9:00, Linda puts on her uniform and goes to the hospital again. But Linda wants to change her hours of work soon.

1. Where/Linda/live?

Where does Linda live? She lives in Toronto.

2. What/Tom/do?

_____

3. How many children/they/have?

_____

4. What/Nancy/do?

_____

5. What/Linda/do?

_____

6. Where/Linda/work?

_____

7. When/Linda/start work?

_____

8. When/Linda/finish work?

_____

9. What/she/do after breakfast?

_____

10. What/they/eat?

_____

11. What/they/do/after dinner?

_____

12. What/they/watch together?

_____

13. What/she/put on?

_____

14. Where/she/go?

_____

15. Why/she/go there?

_____

26 **Your Turn**

Why do you think Linda wants to change her hours?
Give three reasons.

Example:
Because she doesn't see her daughter.

27 Practice

Complete the questions with *is*, *are*, *do*, or *does*.

1. What _____*is*_____ the largest animal on land?

   It's the elephant.

2. Where _____ it live?

   It lives in Africa and Asia.

3. What _____ it eat?

   It eats plants.

4. How long _____ it live?

   It lives for about 70 years.

5. _____ elephants intelligent?

   Yes, they are. Elephants are intelligent.

6. _____ elephants live alone?

   No, they don't. They live in groups.

7. When _____ a female elephant have its first baby?

   It has its first baby when it is 6 years old.

8. How many babies_____ it have?

   It has one baby at one time.

9. How many kinds of elephants_____ there?

   There are two kinds of elephants.

10. What _____ they?

    They are the African elephant and the Indian elephant.

11. _____ an elephant cry?

    Yes, it does. An elephant cries.

12. _____ elephants laugh?

    Yes, they do. Elephants laugh.

Practice

Write questions for these answers about pandas.

1. _What color is a panda_ ?

   A panda is black and white.

2. _____ ?

   It lives in China.

3. _____ ?

   It eats bamboo.

4. _____ ?

   Yes, it eats only bamboo.

5. _____ ?

   There are about 1,000 pandas in the world.

6. _____ ?

   A panda lives for about 15 years.

7. _____ ?

   No, they don't. Pandas don't sleep in winter.

8. _____ ?

   Yes, they do. Pandas usually live alone.

Read the answers. Then write the questions.

Louisa

Gina

1. *Is Gina Louisa's sister*   ?

   Yes, she is. (Gina is Louisa's sister.)

2. _____?

   Gina is twenty-eight.

3. _____?

   Gina works for Channel AB on television. She gives the news.

4. _____?

   Yes, she is famous.

5. _____?

   She lives in Los Angeles.

6. _____?

   Yes, she's married to a TV producer.

7. _____?

   Yes, she has a daughter.

8. _____?

   No, she isn't happy.

9. _____?

   She's unhappy because she has no time for her husband and her daughter.

10. _____?

Yes, she often talks to her sister Louisa on the phone.

11. _____?

Yes, Louisa is happy.

12. _____?

No, Louisa is not famous.

13. _____?

She lives at home with her parents.

14. _____?

No, she doesn't work. She's a student.

30 Your Turn

A. Ask your partner questions with *what, where, when, who, how,* and *why* about his/her weekends. Use the following verbs or use your own.

do	get up	have breakfast	see
eat	go	have lunch	

Example:
You: What do you do on Saturday nights?
Your partner: I often go to a movie.

B. Write five things that your partner said.

Example:
Tomiko often goes to the movies.

1. _____.

2. _____.

3. _____.

4. _____.

5. _____.

WRITING: Describe a Person

Write a paragraph about another person.

Step 1. Find out about a partner. Ask questions. These prompts may help you.

1. Where do you come from?
2. Where do you live?
3. Do you have brothers or sisters?
4. Do you live alone? Who do you live with?
5. What sports do you like?
6. What language(s) do you speak?
7. What kind of music do you like?

8. What time do you get up?
9. What do you have for breakfast?
10. What do you usually have for lunch?
11. When do you go home?
12. What do you do in the evening?
13. When do you go to bed?

Step 2. Write the answers to the questions from Step 1.

Step 3. Rewrite your answers in paragraph form. Write a title (your partner's name). For more writing guidelines, see pages 202-207.

> Belén Gutierrez
>
> Belén Gutierrez comes from Buenos Aires, Argentina, but now she lives in Las Vegas, Nevada, in the United States. She has...

Step 4. Evaluate your paragraph.

Checklist

_____ Did you indent the first line?
_____ Did you give your paragraph a title?
_____ Did you write the title with a capital letter for each word?

Step 5. Edit your work. Work with a partner to edit your paragraph. Correct spelling, punctuation, vocabulary, and grammar.

Step 6. Write your final copy.

SELF-TEST

A   **Choose the best answer, A, B, C, or D, to complete the sentence. Mark your answer by darkening the oval with the same letter.**

1. It _____ in Hawaii.

    A. often rain   Ⓐ Ⓑ Ⓒ Ⓓ
    B. often rains
    C. rain often
    D. rains often

2. Brazilians _____ Portuguese.

    A. speak   Ⓐ Ⓑ Ⓒ Ⓓ
    B. speaks
    C. is speaking
    D. do speaks

3. The United States _____ fifty states.

    A. have   Ⓐ Ⓑ Ⓒ Ⓓ
    B. is have
    C. has
    D. does

4. Crocodiles _____ in cold countries.

    A. doesn't live   Ⓐ Ⓑ Ⓒ Ⓓ
    B. live not
    C. isn't live
    D. don't live

5. When _____?

    A. is summer start   Ⓐ Ⓑ Ⓒ Ⓓ
    B. does summer start
    C. start summer
    D. does start summer

6. _____ a fish _____?

    A. Does ... sleep   Ⓐ Ⓑ Ⓒ Ⓓ
    B. Do ... sleeps
    C. Don't ... sleep
    D. Is ... sleep

7. Where _____?

    A. does coffee come from   Ⓐ Ⓑ Ⓒ Ⓓ
    B. coffee come from
    C. is coffee come from
    D. coffee comes from

8. Whales give milk to _____ young.

    A. her   Ⓐ Ⓑ Ⓒ Ⓓ
    B. they
    C. their
    D. its

9. It _____ cold in Antarctica.

    A. is always   Ⓐ Ⓑ Ⓒ Ⓓ
    B. always is
    C. does always
    D. always has

10. What _____?

    A. is "fetch" mean   Ⓐ Ⓑ Ⓒ Ⓓ
    B. "fetch" mean
    C. does "fetch" mean
    D. does means "fetch"

B **Find the underlined word or phrase, A, B, C, or D, that is incorrect. Mark your answer by darkening the oval with the same letter.**

1. <u>Chinese people</u> <u>usually</u> <u>celebrates</u> the
        A   B   C

    New Year <u>in February.</u>
              D

    Ⓐ Ⓑ Ⓒ Ⓓ

2. <u>Do</u> elephants <u>lives</u> in groups, <u>or</u> <u>do they</u>
     A   B   C   D

    live alone?

    Ⓐ Ⓑ Ⓒ Ⓓ

3. The male lion <u>is</u> very lazy, <u>and</u> <u>sleep</u> for
             A   B   C

    about twenty <u>hours</u> a day.
                D

    Ⓐ Ⓑ Ⓒ Ⓓ

4. Babies <u>doesn't</u> <u>have</u> tears when they
           A   B

    <u>cry</u> until they <u>are</u> several weeks old.
     C   D

    Ⓐ Ⓑ Ⓒ Ⓓ

5. <u>Giraffes</u> <u>don't sometimes</u> <u>sleep</u> at all
     A   B   C

    <u>for twenty-four hours.</u>
         D

    Ⓐ Ⓑ Ⓒ Ⓓ

6. <u>People</u> <u>in the</u> United States <u>use often</u>
      A   B   C

    <u>credit cards.</u>
      D

    Ⓐ Ⓑ Ⓒ Ⓓ

7. July <u>has</u> cold <u>in Argentina</u>, <u>but</u> <u>it's</u> warm
        A   B   C D

    in New York.

    Ⓐ Ⓑ Ⓒ Ⓓ

8. When <u>do people</u> <u>have the flu</u>, they <u>usually</u>
         A   B   C

    <u>have a temperature.</u>
        D

    Ⓐ Ⓑ Ⓒ Ⓓ

9. <u>Gorillas</u> <u>rarely</u> <u>climb</u> trees because of <u>its</u>
     A   B   C   D

    size.

    Ⓐ Ⓑ Ⓒ Ⓓ

10. <u>How many</u> <u>babies</u> <u>does</u> a panda <u>has</u>?
       A   B   C   D

    Ⓐ Ⓑ Ⓒ Ⓓ

UNIT 4

THE PRESENT PROGRESSIVE TENSE

Form

A: That girl **is looking** at me!

B: Which one?

A: She **is wearing** a hat, and she **is drinking** a soda.

We form the present progressive (also called the present continuous) with the present of the verb *to be* and the base verb + *ing*.

Subject	Be	Base Verb + *-ing*
I	**am**	
You	**are**	
He		
She	**is**	**working.**
It		
We		
You	**are**	
They		

We use the present progressive to talk about what is happening now.

The students **are studying** in the library now.
They **are reading.**

It **is snowing** right now.
The woman **is smiling.**

1 Practice

It's Sunday. You are looking out of the window. Complete the sentences with the present progressive tense of the verb in parentheses.

1. The birds _____are singing_____ (sing).

2. Tony _____ (work) in the yard.

3. Fred and Tom _____ (talk) in the street.

4. A child _____ (eat) ice cream.

5. Children _____ (play) in the park.

6. Bob _____ (wash) his car.

7. A woman _____ (walk) in the street.

8. A cat _____ (sleep) in a tree.

9. Maria _____ (clean) the windows.

10. Bob and Linda _____ (go) to the car.

11. Alex _____ (fix) his motorbike.

12. Jo _____ (do) his homework.

13. Carol _____ (read) the newspaper.

14. A man _____ (wait) for the bus.

15. A boy _____ (stand) by a tree.

16. He _____ (drink) a soda.

17. Two girls _____ (watch) the boy.

18. The girls _____ (wear) jeans.

19. The girls _____ (walk).

20. An airplane _____ (fly) in the sky.

2 | Practice

Look at the photos. Write the correct sentence in the blanks under the pictures.

Linda is talking on the phone.

The girl is reading a book.

Ted is opening the door.

Peter is carrying bags and suitcases.

Hugo is painting a picture.

The girls are eating ice cream.

The baby is crying.

Paul is playing the guitar.

1. _Paul is playing the_
   guitar .

2. _____
   _____ .

3. _____

_____.

4. _____

_____.

5. _____

_____.

6. _____

_____.

7. _____

_____.

8. _____

_____.

3 Practice

Look at these two old photos. Talk about the man and the woman in the photos. Then write sentences using the words from the list.

Nouns

hat	coat	shirt	skirt	tie
boots	hat	shoes	suit	umbrella

Verbs

carry   stand   wear

1. He   *He's wearing a shirt* _____ .
2. She _____ .
3. She _____ .
4. He _____ .
5. She _____ .
6. He _____ .
7. She _____ .
8. He _____ .
9. He _____ .
10. They _____ .

4 Practice

Work with a partner or the class. Describe what a student in your class is wearing. Do not say the name of the student. Do not say *he* or *she*. Say "the student." Can your partner or the class guess who it is?

Example:

You:	The student is wearing black shoes.
Your partner:	Is it Kang?
You:	No, it isn't. The person is wearing a sweater.

4b The Spelling of Verbs Ending in *-ing*

Form

The sun is shi**ning.**

The woman is si**tting** on a chair by the beach.

She is ty**ping** on her laptop.

Verb Ending	Rule	Examples	
1. Consonant + *e.*	Drop the *e*, add *–ing*.	dance	danc**ing**
		come	com**ing**
2. One vowel + consonant.	Double the consonant, add *–ing*.	sit	sit**ting**
Exception: Verbs that end in *w, x, y.*	Do not double *w, x, y*.	show	show**ing**
		fix	fix**ing**
		say	say**ing**
3. Two vowels + one consonant.	Do not double the consonant. Add *-ing*.	eat	**eating**
		sleep	sleep**ing**
4. All other verbs.	Add *-ing*	talk	talk**ing**
		read	read**ing**

Vowels: a, e, i, o, u
Consonants: b, c, d, f, g, h, j, k, l, m, n, p, q, r, s, t, v, w, x, y, z

5 Practice

Write the base form of each verb.

1. saving _____save_____
2. making _____
3. typing _____
4. writing _____
5. studying _____
6. relaxing _____
7. hoping _____
8. planning _____
9. adding _____
10. trying _____

11. raining _____
12. smiling _____
13. hurrying _____
14. kissing _____
15. riding _____
16. driving _____
17. agreeing _____
18. giving _____
19. swimming_____
20. standing _____

6 Practice

Use the rules for adding –ing to the verbs in the list. Then write them in the correct column.

cry	move	run	wash
dance	play	save	wear
fix	put	smile	
get	rain	stop	
hope	read	take	

Add *-ing*	Drop *e*, add *–ing*	Double the consonant, add *–ing*
crying	*dancing*	*getting*

7 Practice

Fill in the blank with the present progressive of the verb in parentheses. Use the correct spelling.

Dear Elsie,

It's Monday evening and it (rain) _____*is raining*_____ outside. I

(sit) _____ at my desk in my room. I (watch) _____
         2   3
the rain from my window, and I (think) _____ of you. All the family is at
                                           4
home this evening. My father (read) _____ a book and
                                          5
(eat) _____ popcorn. My brother (play) _____
         6   7
video games in his room. My mother is in the kitchen. She (make) _____
                                                                      8
a cake because it's my sister's birthday tomorrow. Right now my sister is in her room. She

(do) _____ her homework, and she (listen to) _____
         9   10
music at the same time. The telephone (ring) _____, and my mother
                                                11
(call) _____ me. I must go now.
         12
Write soon,

Magda

8 Practice

Write eight sentences about what is happening in your class right now. Use the verbs in the list or use your own.

listen	read	stand	wear
look at	sit	talk to	write

1. *The teacher is standing in front of the class* _____ .
2. _____ .
3. _____ .
4. _____ .
5. _____ .
6. _____ .
7. _____ .
8. _____ .

4c The Present Progressive Tense: Negative Statements

The man **is not sleeping.**

He**'s not sleeping.**

OR

He **isn't sleeping.**

To form the negative of the present progressive tense, we use **not** after the verb **be** and the verb + *ing*. There are two forms of contractions. Both forms of contraction are correct:

are not = **'re not**   OR   **aren't**
is not = **'s not**   OR   **isn't**

Subject	Be	Not	Base Verb + -ing	Contraction
I	**am**			**I'm not.***
You	**are**			You**'re not/aren't.**
He				He**'s not/isn't.**
She	**is**	**not**	**working.**	She**'s not/isn't.**
It				It**'s not/isn't.**
We	**are**			We**'re not/aren't.**
They				They**'re not/aren't.**

* There is no contraction for *am not*.

9 Practice

Look at Photo A. Read the statements. Write correct negative and affirmative statements.

Photo A

1. The man and the woman are standing in an office. *The man and the woman aren't standing in an office. They are standing in the street.*

2. The man is talking on the phone. _____

3. The man is holding an umbrella. _____

4. The man is looking at the cars. _____

5. The man is wearing a raincoat. _____

6. The woman is holding her handbag. _____

7. It is raining. The sun isn't shining. _____

8. The woman is working on her computer. _____

Look at Photo A in Exercise 9 and Photo B below. What is different in Photo B?
Write affirmative and negative statements using the present progressive tense.

Photo B

1. *The woman isn't talking on the telephone*   .

2. _____ .

3. _____ .

4. _____ .

5. _____ .

6. _____ .

4d The Present Progressive Tense: Yes/No Questions

Form

A: **Is** the woman **riding** her bicycle?

B: No, **she isn't.**

A: **Is** she **standing** next to her bicycle?

B: Yes, **she is.**

YES/NO QUESTIONS			SHORT ANSWERS	
Be	**Subject**	**Base Verb + *-ing***	**Affirmative**	**Negative**
			Yes,	**No,**
Am	I		you **are.**	you**'re not/aren't.**
Are	you		I **am.**	I'**m not.**
Is	he	working now?	he **is.**	he'**s not/isn't.**
	she		she **is.**	she'**s not/isn't.**
	it		it **is.**	it'**s not/isn't.**
Are	we		you **are.**	you'**re not/aren't.**
	you		we **are.**	we'**re not/aren't.**
	they		they **are.**	they'**re not/aren't.**

11 Practice

Match the questions with the answers.

<u> d </u> **1.** Is your sister studying?

_____ **2.** Is the sun shining?

_____ **3.** Am I taking your seat?

_____ **4.** Are you studying?

_____ **5.** Is David cooking?

_____ **6.** Are the children sleeping?

a. No, you're not. That seat is free.

b. Yes, they are. They're in their beds.

c. Yes, he is. He's making rice.

d. No, she isn't. She's watching television.

e. Yes, we are. We're learning grammar.

f. No, it's not. It's cloudy.

12 Practice

Look at the photo. Ask and answer questions as in the example.

1. (the bride/wear a white dress)

A: Is the bride wearing a white dress _____?

B: Yes, she is _____.

2. (the bride/hold flowers)

_____?

_____.

3. (the bride/smile)

_____?

_____.

4. (the mother/stand next to the groom)

_____?

_____.

5. (the people/sit)

_____?

_____.

6. (the father/wear a suit)

_____?

_____.

7. (the groom/wear a flower on his jacket)

_____?

_____.

8. (the mother/cry)

_____?

_____.

9. (the mother and father/hold hands)

_____?

_____.

10. (the mother and father/wear hats)

_____?

_____.

Work with a partner or the class. Take the role of a person in one of the photos in this unit. Your partner or the class ask you yes/no questions to find out which person you are.

Example:
You: Are you getting married?
Your partner: No, I'm not.
You: Are you standing next to your bicycle?
Your partner: Yes, I am.

4e The Present Progressive Tense: Wh- Questions

Form

A: **What** is the man doing?
B: He's talking on the phone and walking.
A: **Where** is he walking?
B: He's walking down the street.

Wh- Word	*Be*	Subject	Base Verb + *-ing*
Where	**is**	Tony	**working?**
What	**are**	you	**eating?**
Why	**is**	Susan	**studying?**
When	**are**	they	**coming?**
Who*	**is**	Ken	**talking** to?
How	**are**	you	**feeling?**

* In formal written English, the wh-word would be *whom*.

Write a question for each sentence. Use the wh- question words in parentheses.

1. She's watching a movie. (what)

   What is she watching ?

2. I am drinking tea. (what)

   _____?

3. He is going to the store. (where)

   _____?

4. Sandra is coming at six. (when)

   _____?

5. I am taking an umbrella because it is raining. (why)

   _____?

6. Peter is talking to his father. (who)

   _____?

7. Linda is feeling fine. (how)

   _____?

8. The children are playing in the park. (where)

   _____?

9. She is going to the bank this afternoon. (when)

   _____?

10. I am talking to Bill on the telephone. (who)

   _____?

Practice

Look at the pictures and write questions for the sentences. The underlined words are the answers.

Items 1-4

Items 5-8

1. The children are looking at <u>their teacher</u>.

   Who are the children looking at _____ ?

2. <u>The children</u> are sitting at their desks.

   _____ ?

3. They are sitting <u>in chairs</u>.

   _____ ?

4. They are holding their hands <u>in the air</u>.

   _____ ?

5. The man and the woman <u>are eating</u>. (Use *doing* in your question.)

   _____ ?

6. They are sitting <u>in a restaurant</u>.

   _____ ?

7. They are eating <u>salads</u>.

   _____ ?

8. They are feeling <u>happy</u>.

   _____ ?

4f Verbs Not Used in the Present Progressive Tense

I **love** Paris. I **think** Paris is beautiful.

1. Some verbs are not usually used in the present progressive tense. These are called nonaction verbs. They describe a state or condition, not an action. We use the simple present with these verbs.

Nonaction Verbs			
believe	know	prefer	taste
hate	like	remember	think
have	love	see	understand
hear	need	smell	want

CORRECT: I **know** the answer.
INCORRECT: I am knowing the answer.

CORRECT: Do you **hear** the music?
INCORRECT: Are you hearing the music?

2. The verbs *think* and *have* are sometimes used in the present progressive tense.

He **thinks** it is difficult. ("Think" here means "believe.")
He **is thinking** about his family. ("Think" here means "thoughts are going through the person's mind.")

Julia **has** a car. ("Has" here means "possess.")
We **are having** a good time. (In certain idiomatic expressions, such as **have a good/bad time** and **have a problem/difficulty**, *have* can be used in the progressive tenses.)

16 Practice

Look at the following pairs. Only one sentence is possible. Check the correct sentence.

1. _____ a. Mary is having a lot of work right now.

   _✓_ b. Mary has a lot of work right now.

2. _____ a. Susan needs a new coat.

   _____ b. Susan is needing a new coat.

3. _____ a. Look! That man takes a photo of us.

   _____ b. Look! That man is taking a photo of us.

4. _____ a. Please be quiet. I study.

   _____ b. Please be quiet. I am studying.

5. _____ a. This cup of coffee is smelling good.

   _____ b. This cup of coffee smells good.

6. _____ a. I look for a new apartment.

   _____ b. I'm looking for a new apartment.

7. _____ a. The children are loving ice cream.

   _____ b. The children love ice cream.

8. _____ a. He's not understanding Japanese.

   _____ b. He doesn't understand Japanese.

17 Practice

Complete the dialogue with the simple present or present progressive of the verb in parentheses.

Maria: Where (go) _are_ you _going_ ?
                        1   2

Tony: I (go) _____ to the store.
                    3

Maria: But it (rain) _____ outside.
                      4

Tony: I (know) _____ . I (love) _____ the rain.
                    5   6

       (want) _____ you _____ anything from the store?
               7   8

Maria: Yes. I (need) _____ a notepad for my homework.
                     9

Tony: O.K. What color? White or yellow?

Maria: I (prefer) _____ white. Thanks, Tony.
                10

18 Practice

Look at the photo and complete the sentences with the correct form of the verbs from the list. You may use a verb more than one time. Use the simple present or present progressive.

have   sit   wear   read   love   buy

The woman in the picture _____*has*_____ long hair. She _____ a

2

white blouse and a skirt. In the picture, she _____ at a table in a

3

restaurant. She _____ a book. She _____ some flowers.

4   5

She _____ flowers, so she _____ flowers from the flower

6   7

market every week.

19 Your Turn

What three things do you hear right now?
What three things do you see right now?
What three things do you have right now?

Example:
I hear the radio, the traffic outside, and a dog barking.

4g The Simple Present Tense and the Present Progressive Tense

Sally **is stretching** right now.

Sally **stretches** every day.

The Simple Present	The Present Progressive
Statements Use the simple present for actions you do all the time or again and again. I **watch** television every evening. He **studies** grammar every day.	**Statements** Use the present progressive for an action happening right now. I **am watching** television right now. He**'s studying** grammar at the moment.
Questions Use *do* and *does* plus the base verb. **Do** you watch television every day? **Does** he study grammar every day?	**Questions** Use *am*, *is*, or *are* plus the *-ing* verb. **Are** you watching television right now? **Is** he studying grammar at the moment?
Negatives Use *do* and *does* plus *not* and the base verb. I **don't** watch television every day. He **doesn't** study grammar every day.	**Negatives** Use *am*, *is*, or *are* plus *not* and the *-ing* verb. I**'m not** watching television right now. He **isn't** studying grammar at the moment.

Function

The Simple Present Tense	The Present Progressive Tense
We use the simple present to talk about things that people do all the time or again and again. I **run** three times a week.	We use the present progressive to talk about things that are happening right now. She's **running** now.

20 Practice

Complete the sentences with the words in parentheses. Use contractions when possible.

A.

A: What are you doing? (study) _Are_ you _studying_ ?
   ₁   ₂

B: No, I (study, not) _____. I
                              ₃

   (clean) _____ my car.
                   ₄

A: (wash) _____ you _____ your car every week?
          ₅   ₆

B: Yes, I (like) _____ a clean car.
                           ₇

B.

A: Why (sit) _____ you _____ in front of the class? You usually
            ₁   ₂

   (sit) _____ at the back.
                   ₃

B: I know. I (not, have) _____ my glasses with me today.
                                  ₄

C.

   Paul (sit) _____ at his desk at the office.
                       ₁

He (talk) _____ on the phone. His boss is angry. Paul always
                  ₂

(talk) _____ on the phone with his friends.
               ₃

He (not, like) _____ to work.
                       ₄

D.

A: (speak) _____ you _____ Japanese?
           ₁   ₂

B: Yes, I (speak) _____ a little.
                          ₃

A: What (mean) _____ "mushi mushi" _____?
              ₄   ₅

B: It (mean) _____ "hello."
                     ₆

E.

A: How often (write) _____ you _____ to your family?
                     ₁   ₂

B: I (not, like) _____ to write letters. I
                         ₃

   (call) _____ them every week.
                  ₄

F.

A: Look at Bob! He (watch) _____ television again, and
   1

   he's (not, do) _____ his homework!
   2

B: (watch) _____ he _____ television every night?
   3   4

A: Yes, he (watch) _____ it for four hours every night!
   5

G.

A: (go) _____ you _____ out now?
   1   2

B: Yes, I (go) _____ to the store. (need) _____ you
   3   4

   _____ anything?
   5

A: I (not, know) _____ right now.
   6

H.

A: (work) _____ you _____ at the moment?
   1   2

B: Yes, I (sit) _____ at my desk right now.
   3

A: (like) _____ you _____ it?
   4   5

B: Yes, I (love) _____ it. I
   6

   (write) _____ for five hours every day.
   7

I.

A: Why (put) _____ you _____ on your coat?
   1   2

B: I (go) _____ for a walk. (want) _____ you
   3   4

   _____ to come with me?
   5

J.

A: What (usually, have) _____ you _____ for breakfast?
   1   2

B: I (usually, have) _____ cereal and a cup of coffee. But
   3

   I (eat) _____ toast now.
   4

K.

A: What (wait) _____ you _____ for?
               1   2

B: I (wait) _____ for the store to open.
                       3

A: But it (open) _____ at ten every day.
                          4

B: I (know) _____ . I (want) _____
                   5   6

   to be early. The sale starts today.

L.

A: Why (walk) _____ you _____ so fast? You usually
             1   2

   (not, walk) _____ fast.
                    3

B: I (hurry) _____ because my father
                  4

   (wait) _____ for me.
               5

M.

A: (usually, take) _____ you _____ the bus to school?
                 1   2

B: Yes, I (always, take) _____ the bus. I
                          3

   (like) _____ it. I
                 4

   (not, have) _____ a problem with parking.
                    5

N.

A: (remember) _____ you _____ Joanne?
               1   2

B: Yes. (still, study) _____ she _____?
                 3   4

A: No. She (work) _____ now. She
                  5

   (have) _____ a very good job in a hospital.
              6

O.

A: (have) _____ you _____ Bob Bradley's telephone number?
            1   2

B: Yes, I (have) _____ his number, but it's at home.
                  3

A: Oh, no! I really (need) _____ his number right now.
                        4

21

Your Turn

A. Think of someone you know very well. Tell your partner three things that the person is doing now. If you are not sure, you can use *maybe* or *probably*. Then tell your partner five things that the person does regularly.

Example:
Maybe he is having lunch now.
He is probably having lunch now.
He always has lunch at 1:00.

B. Write sentences that tell about the person that your partner talked about.

Example:
Her friend is having lunch now.

1. _____.
2. _____.
3. _____.
4. _____.
5. _____.
6. _____.
7. _____.
8. _____.

Write a postcard about a vacation.

Step 1. Read the postcard and answer the questions.

Dear Pam,

    We are here in Hawaii on the island of Oahu. We're having a great time. We're staying in a big hotel on Waikiki beach. I'm writing this postcard in the hotel you see in the picture. My husband, Tony, is lying on the beach, and little Jerry is swimming in the pool. We're enjoying the vacation very much.

See you soon!

    Rima, Tony, and Jerry

Pam Leed
250 Orchard Avenue
Apple Valley, California
U.S.A. 98000

1. Who is writing the postcard?
2. Where are they staying?
3. Where are they writing the card from?

4. What are Tony and Jerry doing?
5. Are they enjoying the vacation?

Step 2. Check your answers with a partner.

Step 3. Now write a postcard to a friend. Use your own information. Use the postcard in Step 1 to help you. Tell about these things. For more writing guidelines see pages 202-207.

1. where you are
2. where you are staying
3. where you are writing the card

4. what you and your family are doing
5. if you are enjoying the vacation

Step 4. Edit your work. Work with a partner to edit your paragraph. Correct spelling, punctuation, vocabulary, and grammar.

Step 5. Write your final copy.

SELF-TEST

A **Choose the best answer, A, B, C, or D, to complete the sentence. Mark your answer by darkening the oval with the same letter.**

1. We _____ oxygen to live.

    A. needs   Ⓐ Ⓑ Ⓒ Ⓓ
    B. needing
    C. need
    D. are needing

2. Schools _____ in tests.

    A. believing   Ⓐ Ⓑ Ⓒ Ⓓ
    B. is believing
    C. are believing
    D. believe

3. This food _____ delicious.

    A. smelling   Ⓐ Ⓑ Ⓒ Ⓓ
    B. is smelling
    C. smells
    D. smell

4. I _____ my first day at school.

    A. remembering   Ⓐ Ⓑ Ⓒ Ⓓ
    B. remember
    C. am remembering
    D. to remember

5. It _____ right now.

    A. not rain   Ⓐ Ⓑ Ⓒ Ⓓ
    B. does not rain
    C. not raining
    D. is not raining

6. I _____ on the phone right now.

    A. talk   Ⓐ Ⓑ Ⓒ Ⓓ
    B. talking
    C. am talking
    D. be talking

7. What _____ here?

    A. you are doing   Ⓐ Ⓑ Ⓒ Ⓓ
    B. you doing
    C. are you doing
    D. you do

8. We _____ English in class.

    A. are always speaking   Ⓐ Ⓑ Ⓒ Ⓓ
    B. always speak
    C. speak always
    D. are speaking always

9. Foreign students _____ some American customs.

    A. do not understand   Ⓐ Ⓑ Ⓒ Ⓓ
    B. do no understand
    C. no understand
    D. are not understanding

10. _____ the music?

    A. Are you hearing   Ⓐ Ⓑ Ⓒ Ⓓ
    B. You are hearing
    C. Do you hear
    D. You hear

B   **Find the underlined word or phrase, A, B, C, or D, that is incorrect. Mark your answer by darkening the oval with the same letter.**

1. Hippos <u>are eating</u> <u>at night,</u> <u>and</u> <u>spend</u>
          A   B   C   D

    the day in the water.

    Ⓐ Ⓑ Ⓒ Ⓓ

2. <u>Fingernails</u> <u>growing</u> more during <u>the day</u>
        A   B   C

    than <u>at night.</u>
          D

    Ⓐ Ⓑ Ⓒ Ⓓ

3. Bears <u>do not</u> see well so <u>they</u> <u>smelling</u>
          A   B   C

    <u>their</u> food.
     D

    Ⓐ Ⓑ Ⓒ Ⓓ

4. Many people <u>are thinking</u> the heart <u>is</u> on
                 A   B

    the left, but <u>it</u> <u>is</u> in the middle of your
               C D

    chest.

    Ⓐ Ⓑ Ⓒ Ⓓ

5. <u>Sometimes</u> students <u>having</u> <u>problems</u>
        A   B   C

    with <u>English</u> spelling.
         D

    Ⓐ Ⓑ Ⓒ Ⓓ

6. Teachers <u>in the United States</u> <u>are</u> <u>not</u>
         A   B   C   D

    <u>wear</u> uniforms.

    Ⓐ Ⓑ Ⓒ Ⓓ

7. We <u>freeze</u> here in New York right now,
          A

    and <u>people</u> <u>are lying</u> in the sun in
          B   C

    <u>Australia.</u>
       D

    Ⓐ Ⓑ Ⓒ Ⓓ

8. When <u>does</u> the semester <u>ending,</u> <u>in</u>
          A   B   C

    June <u>or</u> July?
        D

    Ⓐ Ⓑ Ⓒ Ⓓ

9. <u>Are</u> you <u>need</u> <u>a dictionary</u> <u>for the test</u>?
      A   B   C   D

    Ⓐ Ⓑ Ⓒ Ⓓ

10. The students <u>are</u> not <u>take</u> a test right
                 A   B

    now, they <u>are waiting</u> for <u>their</u> teacher.
              C   D

    Ⓐ Ⓑ Ⓒ Ⓓ

UNIT 5

NOUNS AND PRONOUNS

5a Count and Noncount Nouns

Tom: What's on the pizza?
Karen: **Tomatoes, peppers, garlic, cheese, and olives.**
Tom: No **mushrooms?**

1. We can count some things. *Book* is a count noun. It can be singular or plural (one book, two books).

2. We cannot count other nouns. These are noncount nouns. These nouns do not have *a* or *an* in front of them, and they have no plural. Here are some noncount nouns.

Examples of Noncount Nouns	
Mass nouns	cheese, butter, meat, salt, pepper, bread, rice, sugar, money, paper, gold, tea, water, milk, oil, soup, gasoline, wood, silver
Abstract nouns	love, happiness, beauty, luck, peace
Others	advice, furniture, information, weather, help, homework, work, traffic, music

3. Noncount nouns take a singular verb.
   Water **is** important.
   Gold **is** expensive.

1 Practice

Write *C* for count nouns and *N* for noncount nouns.

1. _N_ coffee
2. _____ letter
3. _____ city
4. _____ traffic
5. _____ cheese
6. _____ flower

7. _____ teacher
8. _____ weather
9. _____ banana
10. _____ milk
11. _____ gold
12. _____ meat

13. _____ rice
14. _____ house
15. _____ advice
16. _____ food
17. _____ bed
18. _____ sugar

19. _____ chair
20. _____ money
21. _____ work
22. _____ bread
23. _____ lemon
24. _____ music

Your Turn

Think of six things you find in a supermarket. Then put them into two groups.

	Count		Noncount
1.	apples	4.	milk
2.	_____	5.	_____
3.	_____	6.	_____

5b A/An and *Some*

Function

There is **an** apple. There are **some** cookies, and there's **some** milk.

1. We use *a/an* in front of singular count nouns. Remember, *a* and *an* mean "one."

   a table
   an umbrella

2. We use *some* in front of noncount nouns. *Some* means "a quantity of".

   CORRECT: The cake has **some** milk in it
   INCORRECT: The cake has ~~a milk~~ in it.

3. We also use **some** with count nouns in the plural.

   a book
   some books

   * It is possible to use *milk* as a count noun, but the meaning is different.
   I want a milk. = I want *a serving of* milk.

3 Practice

Tony and Stella are preparing for a picnic. Here's a list of things they need. Complete with *a/an* or *some*.

1. __some__ water
2. _____ orange juice
3. _____ tablecloth
4. _____ radio
5. _____ cups
6. _____ ice chest
7. _____ fruit
8. _____ tent

9. _____ salt
10. _____ sandwiches
11. _____ napkins
12. _____ forks
13. _____ knives
14. _____ umbrella
15. _____ cookies
16. _____ volleyball

4 Practice

What does Joe eat every morning?

He has some coffee. He puts __some__ milk in his coffee. He also puts in
_____ sugar. He has _____ bread. He puts _____ butter on the
   2   3   4
bread. Sometimes he has _____ cheese. He likes _____ fruit in the
                          5   6
morning. He has _____ orange every morning. And he has _____ banana
                  7   8
with _____ cookie at 10:30.
       9

5 Your Turn

What do you have every morning?

Example:
I have some tea.

5c A/An or *The*

There is **a** dog outside. **The** dog is big.

We use *the* with singular count, plural count, and noncount nouns.

He has a car. **The** car is black. (singular count noun)
I have two boys. **The** boys are at school. (plural count noun)
I have some information. **The** information is important. (noncount noun)

Function

1. We use *the* when the person we are speaking to knows which person or thing we are talking about.

    Tony: Where's John?

    Annie: He's in **the** house.

    (Both Tony and Annie know which house they are talking about.)

2. We use *a/an* when the person we are speaking to does not know which person or thing we are talking about. Often, we use *a/an* when we mention something for the first time. We use *the* after that because the other person knows what we are talking about.

    There's **a** dog and **a** cat outside. **The** dog is chasing **the** cat.

6 Practice

Complete the sentences with *the, a,* or *an*.

A.

I live in __*an*__ apartment in the city. _____ apartment is in _____ big building.
  1   2   3
_____ building is old, but it is near transportation and stores. I usually take _____ bus
  4   5
or _____ tramcar to work. _____ bus stops in front of _____ apartment building,
    6   7   8
and _____ tramcar is just _____ hundred yards from _____ building.
      9   10   11

B.

Lisa: Here's _____ letter and _____ postcard for you.
             1   2

Jackie: Where are they from?

Lisa: _____ letter is _____ bill, and _____ postcard is from Ben in Italy.
       3   4   5

Jackie: Just give me _____ postcard, and _____ bill can wait.
                  6   7

C.

     I usually stay at _____ hotel when I go to Mexico City. I always go to _____ same
                      1   2

hotel. It's not _____ expensive hotel, but it's clean. I know _____ owner. He is _____
          3   4   5

nice man. He always gives me _____ good room.
                      6

D.

Don: What do you want to do today?

Kate: I want to see _____ movie.
                1

Don: Which movie?

Kate: There's _____ movie I want to see at _____ movie theater near my house.
         2   3

     I don't know _____ name of the movie. It's about _____ man with _____ dog.
                 4   5   6

     _____ dog has a special ability. It speaks like _____ person.
     7   8

Don: That sounds like _____ silly movie.
                  9

---

7 | Practice

Complete the sentences with *the, a,* or *an*.

A.

Dave: Do you live in __*a*__ house or __*an*__ apartment?
                1   2

James: Well, I have _____ house in the country and _____ apartment in the city.
                3   4

     _____ house was my mother's, and I rent _____ apartment.
     5   6

Dave: Oh. I guess you have _____ car and _____ motorbike, too.
                     7   8

B.

     There were _____ man and _____ woman in the office today. _____ man was
              1   2   3

English. He was tall, and he had _____ moustache. _____ woman was Chinese, I think.
                         4   5

She was _____ well-dressed woman. Here's _____ man's card.
        6   7

C.

When you get to Alexander Avenue, there are four houses: _____ yellow one, _____
₁   ₂

white one, _____ green one, and _____ gray one. I live in _____ gray one. There are
₃   ₄   ₅

two bells on the door: _____ red bell and _____ black bell. Please ring _____ black bell.
₆   ₇   ₈

D.

Timmy: I'm hungry, Mom. Can I have _____ sandwich? _____ egg sandwich would be
     ₁   ₂

       good.

Mom: Sure. Here's _____ egg, and there's _____ tomato in _____ fridge.
     ₃   ₄   ₅

Timmy: Can I also have _____ glass of lemonade?
     ₆

Mom: Sure. _____ lemonade is in _____ fridge, too.
     ₇   ₈

5d   Generalizations

I love **roses.**

1. We do not use *the* when we talk about something in general.

     I smell **roses** in the air.

     Gold is expensive.

2. We use *the* when we are specific.

     The roses in my garden are all red.

     The gold in this jewely is very expensive.

8 Practice

Complete the sentences with *the* or *X* (no article).

1. Amy: What do you like to read about?

   Ken: I love ___X___ history. I really like to read about __*the*__ history of Europe.

2. Ben: Do you watch _____ football on television?

   Steve: No, I don't like _____ football. I like _____ tennis.

3. I don't like _____ meat. I prefer _____ fish. _____ fish at the restaurant was very good.

4. _____ water is very important in our lives. _____ water in this city is bad.

5. I am a vegetarian. I don't eat _____ meat , but I drink _____ milk and eat _____ cheese.

6. Joe: What is important for you: _____ love or _____ money?

   Ben: Well, for me it's _____ love. Especially _____ love I have for my job.

7. _____ life is very difficult when there is no _____ electricity.

8. _____ food in that restaurant is very good. _____ service is good too.

5e *Some* and *Any*

Form

I love this place. I can get **some** peace and quiet here. There aren't **any** cars. There aren't **any** telephones. There isn't **any** noise.

Some: We use *some* in affirmative statements with count and noncount nouns.

I need **some** eggs (count noun) and **some** sugar (noncount noun) to make a cake.

Any: We use *any* in negative statements and questions.

Are there **any** flowers in the park?
No, there **aren't any** flowers. There are some trees.
Is there **any** noise?
No, there **isn't any** noise.

Some: We use *some* to show a quantity when we do not know exactly how much or how many.

 I have **some** time to go on a vacation.

Any: In negative statements and questions, we use *any* to show a quantity when we do not know exactly how much or how many.

 Do you have **any** information?
 Sorry, I don't have **any** information.

9 Practice

Look at the photo and complete the sentences with *some* or *any*.

1. Are there ___any___ cars in the street?

2. No, there aren't _____ cars.

3. Are there _____ buses in the street?

4. No, there aren't _____ buses.

5. Are there _____ bicycles in the street?

6. Yes, there are _____ bicycles.

7. Are there _____ new buildings?

8. No, there aren't _____ new buildings.

9. Are there _____ stores?

10. Yes, there are _____ small stores.

10 What Do You Think?

In what country do you think this street can be? Is it in Europe, North or South America, Asia, or Africa? Why?

11 Practice

Look at the picture. Ask your partner questions with *any*. Your partner answers with *some* or *any*.

Example:
milk
You: Is there **any** milk on the table?
Your partner: Yes, there's **some** milk.

1. bread
2. onions
3. apples
4. rice
5. cheese

6. eggs
7. lemons
8. bananas
9. tomatoes
10. fish

5f Measurement Words

Form

They give you **a glass of** water with **a cup of** coffee.

After measure words we always have a prepositional phrase with *of*.

a cup **of** coffee
a glass **of** water

We use measurement words to count noncount nouns. We also use them with count nouns.

I drink **a cup of** coffee every morning.

Here are some measure words.

a bar of soap	**a can of** tomatoes	**a box of** chocolates
a bunch of bananas	**a tube of** toothpaste	**a glass of** water
a carton of milk	**a sheet of** paper	**a bottle of** wine
a piece of fruit	**a slice of** cake	**a cup of** tea
a head of lettuce	**a pack of** batteries	**a roll of** toilet paper
a jar of jam	**a loaf of** bread	**a bowl of** soup

12 Practice

Suzy is going shopping. She has a list of things she needs to buy. Add measurement words to her list.

1. ___a bar of___ soap
2. _____ toilet paper
3. _____ tomatoes
4. _____ milk
5. _____ bread
6. _____ cereal
7. _____ sugar

8. _____ shampoo
9. _____ batteries
10. _____ toothpaste
11. _____ mayonnaise
12. _____ oil
13. _____ cheese
14. _____ juice

13 Your Turn

How much food do you have at home? Think of six food containers you have. Tell what you have in each container.

Example:
I have a box of cereal.

5g Quantifying Expressions

David runs **a few** miles every day.
He drinks **a lot of** water. He doesn't
drink **any** beer or wine.

	Affirmative	Negative
Count Nouns	There are **many** eggs. There are **a lot of** apples. There are **some** tomatoes. There are **a few** onions.	There aren't **many** eggs. There aren't **a lot of** apples. There aren't **any** tomatoes. There aren't **any** onions. There are **no** onions.
Noncount Nouns	There is **a lot of** juice. There is **some** milk. There is **a little** cheese.	There isn't **much** juice. There isn't **any** milk. There isn't **any** cheese. There is **no** cheese.

Function

1. We use *a lot of* with count and noncount nouns to talk about a large amount or a large number.

    There is **a lot of** food on the table.
    There are **a lot of** apples.

2. We use *a little* with noncount nouns, and we use *a few* with count nouns to talk about a small amount or a small number.

    There is **a little** milk in the carton.
    There are **a few** oranges left.

3. We use *not much* with noncount nouns and *not many* with count nouns to talk about a small amount or a small number.

    There is **not much** coffee.
    There are**n't many** potatoes.

14 Practice

Complete the sentences with _much_ or _many_.

1. David doesn't eat _____much_____ meat.

2. He doesn't eat _____ bread.

3. He eats _____ kinds of cereal.

4. He takes _____ vitamins every day.

5. He doesn't eat _____ eggs.

6. He doesn't drink _____ milk.

7. He doesn't eat _____ cheese.

8. He doesn't eat _____ food at meals.

9. He doesn't use _____ sugar.

10. He doesn't spend _____ money on food.

15 Practice

Complete the sentences with _a few_ or _a little_.

1. He drinks ____a few____ glasses of juice every day.

2. When he is hungry, he eats _____ nuts.

3. He exercises for _____ hours every day.

4. He only uses _____ salt on his food.

5. He also uses _____ oil.

6. He eats _____ fish.

7. He eats _____ oranges every morning.

8. He eats _____ kinds of fruit every day.

16 Your Turn

How much do you eat of these things? Use _a lot of_, _not much_, or _not many_.

Example:
I eat a lot of apples. I don't eat much pasta. I don't eat many cookies.

1. apples	4. pasta	7. meat	10. fish
2. eggs	5. ice cream	8. chocolate	11. fruit
3. rice	6. potatoes	9. bananas	12. bread

Michiko: **How many** slices of bread do
you eat for breakfast?

Tommy: About six.

Michiko: **How much** milk do you drink?

Tommy: Not much. About four glasses.

We use *how many* with plural count nouns. We use *how much* with noncount nouns.

Type of Noun	Wh- Word	Noun	
Plural Count Noun	How many	lemons	do you need?
		friends	do you have?
Noncount Noun	How much	money	do you have?
		milk	is there?

Read about Tommy. Write questions with *how much* and *how many* using the prompts given, and then answer the questions.

> Tommy eats a lot. For breakfast, he goes out to eat. He spends a lot of money on breakfast. He drinks four glasses of milk. He eats four eggs and six slices of bread with a lot of butter and cheese. Then he has a big bowl of cereal. He finishes with four doughnuts and a little coffee.

1. milk/drink *How much milk does he drink*?
   He drinks four glasses of milk.

2. eggs/eat _____?
   _____.

3. slices of bread/eat _____?
   _____.

4. butter and cheese/put on the bread _____?
   _____.

5. cereal/have _____?
   _____.

6. doughnuts/eat _____?
   _____.

7. coffee/drink _____?
   _____.

8. money/spend _____?
   _____.

Ask your partner questions with *how much* or *how many*.

Example:

money do you spend every week

You: How much money do you spend every week?

Your partner: Not much. I just buy food and pay for the bus.

1. money do you spend every week
2. brothers and sisters do you have
3. time do you spend on homework

4. friends do you have
5. money do you save every month
6. hours do you sleep every night

5i *Whose* and Possessive Nouns

Form / Function

Sandra: **Whose** dog is that?

Karen: That's Julia**'s** dog.

WHOSE

1. We use *whose* to ask who owns something or who something belongs to.

Whose	Noun	Verb		Answer with Possessive Nouns
Whose	dog	is	that?	It's Julia**'s** dog. It's her dog. Julia**'s**.
Whose	books	are	these?	They're Ken**'s** books. They're his books. Ken**'s**.

Do not confuse *who's* and *whose*. *Who's* = who is. *Whose* = who owns something.

POSSESSIVE NOUNS

2. We use 's (apostrophe s) or ' (apostrophe) to talk about things that belong to people.

Nouns	Rules	Examples
Singular Nouns	Add an apostrophe + s ('s) to the noun.	It's John**'s** bag. It's the boy**'s** bag.
Regular Plural Nouns (end in –s)	Add an apostrophe to the noun.	They are the boys**'** bags. That's the teachers**'** office.
Irregular Plural Nouns	Add an apostrophe + s ('s) to the noun.	They are the children**'s** toys. They sell women**'s** shoes. That's a men**'s** store.
Names and nouns that already end in s (for example, *Charles, the boss*)	Add apostrophe + s ('s) or an apostrophe (') to the name or noun.	That's Charles**'s** wife OR Charles**'** wife. That's the boss**'s** chair OR the boss**'** chair.

19   Practice

Write questions with *whose* and answer them as in the example.

(bicycle/Mike)

1. *Whose bicycle is this?*
   It's Mike's.
   _____

(sneakers/Ted)

2. _____
   _____
   _____

(hat/Jane)

(house/Sandra)

3. _____

_____

_____

4. _____

_____

_____

(ball/Timmy)

(car/my parents)

5. _____

_____

_____

6. _____

_____

_____

20 Practice

Add ' or 's to the nouns that should show possession. Write the noun in its possessive form in the space to the right.

1. Every Saturday, we go to my mother house for dinner. _____*mother's*_____
2. My parents house is not far, but we take the car. _____
3. I take the children in my husband car. _____
4. I have a girl and a boy. The girl name is Kate. _____
5. The boy name is Andrew. _____
6. Kate hair is red. _____
7. Kate is my mother favorite child. _____
8. My father favorite is Andrew. _____
9. The children favorite day is Saturday. _____
10. They love their grandparents house. _____

21 Practice

Rewrite the questions.

1. What is the name of your teacher? _____*What's your teacher's name*_____?
2. What is the name of your school? _____?
3. What is the name of your partner? _____?
4. What is the name of your best friend? _____?
5. What is the name of your mother/father? _____?
6. What is the address of your mother/father? _____?

22 Your Turn

Write the answers to the questions above.

1. _____*My teacher's name is Mr. Peterson*_____.
2. _____.
3. _____.
4. _____.
5. _____.
6. _____.

Write a descriptive paragraph.

Step 1. Ask and answer questions about what is on the table. Use *how much, how many, a/an, the, a little, a lot, a few, some, any, no,* and so forth.

Example:

You: How many bottles are there?
Your partner: There is one bottle.

Step 2. Write a paragraph about what is on the table. For more writing guidelines, see pages 202-207.

There is a bottle on the table. There is some water in the bottle.

SELF-TEST

A Choose the best answer, A, B, C, or D, to complete the sentence. A dash (–) means that no word is needed to complete the sentence. Mark your answer by darkening the oval with the same letter.

1. I eat _____ every day.

   A. a rice Ⓐ Ⓑ Ⓒ Ⓓ
   B. some rices
   C. some rice
   D. any rice

2. Excuse me, I need _____ information.

   A. any Ⓐ Ⓑ Ⓒ Ⓓ
   B. some
   C. a
   D. an

3. To make a sandwich, you need _____ bread, butter, and cheese.

   A. any Ⓐ Ⓑ Ⓒ Ⓓ
   B. the
   C. a
   D. some

4. How _____ are there in your class?

   A. many students Ⓐ Ⓑ Ⓒ Ⓓ
   B. many student
   C. much students
   D. students many

5. There is _____ bread on the table.

   A. a loaf Ⓐ Ⓑ Ⓒ Ⓓ
   B. a
   C. a loaf of
   D. the loaf of

6. I have _____ umbrella for the rain.

   A. a Ⓐ Ⓑ Ⓒ Ⓓ
   B. an
   C. the
   D. –

7. _____ that man?

   A. Whose Ⓐ Ⓑ Ⓒ Ⓓ
   B. Who
   C. Who is
   D. Is who

8. These are _____ toys.

   A. the children's Ⓐ Ⓑ Ⓒ Ⓓ
   B. a children's
   C. the childrens'
   D. the childs'

9. Those are _____ books.

   A. Ken Ⓐ Ⓑ Ⓒ Ⓓ
   B. Ken's
   C. Kens'
   D. Ken his

10. _____ are big animals.

    A. Elephants Ⓐ Ⓑ Ⓒ Ⓓ
    B. Elephant
    C. The elephants
    D. An elephant

B **Find the underlined word or phrase, A, B, C, or D, that is incorrect. Mark your answer by darkening the oval with the same letter.**

1. A jar of toothpaste sells for about
   A   B

   two dollars these days.
        C   D

   Ⓐ Ⓑ Ⓒ Ⓓ

2. Monkeys don't like to live in cold
   A   B   C

   weathers.
   D

   Ⓐ Ⓑ Ⓒ Ⓓ

3. Many Americans like to eat a bowl of
        A   B

   cereal with a milk for breakfast.
   C   D

   Ⓐ Ⓑ Ⓒ Ⓓ

4. In Great Britain, most people drink tea
                              A   B

   with a few milk in it.
        C   D

   Ⓐ Ⓑ Ⓒ Ⓓ

5. Many Americans are eating more

   chickens, turkey, and fish because too
   A   B   D

   much red meat is not good for them.
            C

   Ⓐ Ⓑ Ⓒ Ⓓ

6. Foods that have a lot of fat, oil, and
                A   B   C

   sugars are not good for you.
   D

   Ⓐ Ⓑ Ⓒ Ⓓ

7. Life was very difficult two hundred years
   A   B

   ago when there was no an electricity.
                    C   D

   Ⓐ Ⓑ Ⓒ Ⓓ

8. Some people take a little vitamins every
   A   B   C

   day; other people don't like to take

   vitamins.
   D

   Ⓐ Ⓑ Ⓒ Ⓓ

9. Walt Disneys' movies and his cartoon
   A   B   C

   characters are popular for children around
                              D

   the world.

   Ⓐ Ⓑ Ⓒ Ⓓ

10. Vegetarians don't eat meat, and some
    A

    vegetarians don't eat cheeses or eggs and
                          B   C

    don't drink milk.
                D

    Ⓐ Ⓑ Ⓒ Ⓓ

UNIT 6

THE SIMPLE PAST TENSE

6a The Simple Past Tense: Regular Verbs

Erika **worked** in a hospital last year.

She **helped** a lot of people.

To form the simple past of regular verbs, add –ed to the base verb. The past form is the same for all persons.

Subject	Base Verb + -ed
I	
You	
He/She/It	work**ed.**
We	
They	

It **rained** yesterday.

He **needed** an umbrella.

1. We use the simple past to talk about actions and situations that began and ended in the past.
2. We can use specific time expressions like *yesterday*, *last week*, and *at three o'clock* with the simple past.

1 Practice

Complete the sentences with the simple past tense of the verbs in parentheses.

1. It _____*rained*_____ (rain) yesterday.

2. Peter _____ (wait) for the bus for 30 minutes.

3. He _____ (walk) into the office at 9:10. He was late.

4. First he _____ (open) the windows.

5. Then he _____ (listen) to his voicemail messages.

6. He _____ (talk) to customers for several hours.

7. Then he _____ (work) on his computer.

8. At 12:15, he was hungry. So he _____ (phone) a restaurant.

9. He _____ (order) a sandwich and a cup of coffee.

10. He _____ (stay) in the office until 5:15 as usual.

11. Peter then _____ (call) a taxi to the airport.

12. He _____ (board) the plane in Boston, and he

    _____ (arrive) in Rio de Janeiro, Brazil.

2 What Do You Think?

We have no news from Peter. Where do you think he is? What do you think he is doing? Write two sentences to tell where he is now and what he is doing.

Example:
Peter is visiting his father. He is very sick.
Peter is meeting an important customer in Brazil. The customer has questions for Peter.

3 Practice

Complete the sentences with the simple present or the simple past of the verbs in parentheses.

1. Three years ago, Trisha (work) _____*worked*_____ at a bakery.

2. Now, she (work) _____ in a bank.

3. Every day, customers (call) _____ her on the phone.

4. Yesterday, she (receive) _____ 75 phone calls.

5. She always (listen) _____ to the customers very carefully.

6. Usually, Trisha (answer) _____ their questions quickly, but last week, somebody (ask) _____ her a difficult question.

7. She (not, be) _____ sure of the answer.

8. On Tuesdays after work, Trisha (play) _____ baseball in the park, but last Tuesday, she (stay) _____ at work late to find the answer to that difficult question.

9. She finally (solve) _____ the problem.

10. Then, last Wednesday, she (call) _____ the customer back with the answer.

4 Your Turn

Work with a partner. What did you do last week? Use the phrases from the list for ideas. Then tell your partner.

watch television	talk to my relatives	stay up late
play a sport/game	work on homework	visit friends
cook dinner	listen to music (say what kind)	clean my apartment

Example:
Last week, I talked to my uncle on the phone.

6b Past Time Expressions

It snowed **three weeks ago.**
It also snowed **last winter.**

PAST TIME EXPRESSIONS		
Yesterday	**Last**	**Ago**
yesterday	last night	five minutes ago
yesterday morning	last week	two hours ago
yesterday afternoon	last month	three days ago
yesterday evening	last year	four weeks ago

Function

1. *Yesterday, last,* and *... ago* tell us when an action happened in the past. We use these words in the following ways.

yesterday	morning, afternoon, and evening
last	night, general periods of time (week, month, year), days of the week, and seasons (summer, winter, spring, fall)
ago	specific lengths of time, for example, five minutes ago

2. Time expressions usually come at the beginning or at the end of a sentence. When they come at the beginning of a sentence, we use a comma after the time expressions.

> **Yesterday morning,** I walked to school.
> OR   I walked to school **yesterday morning.**

5 | Practice

Complete the conversation with *yesterday, last,* or *ago.*

Pamela: Where were you? I called you four times _____*last*_____ week.
1

Meg: I was in New York. I was there for a conference. It started _____
2

Monday and ended _____ .
3

Pamela: Lucky you. I love New York in the fall. I was there two years

_____ in October. The weather was beautiful!
4

Meg: Well, this October was terrible. The rain started two weeks

_____ and stopped _____ week for just two days.
5   6

Then it started to rain again _____ afternoon just as I arrived at
7

the airport.

Pamela: _____ afternoon? Were you in that traffic jam at the airport?
8

Meg: Yes, I was. I was really tired _____ night when I got home. I was
9

in bed by nine and opened my eyes only an hour _____.
10

Pamela: Oh, I called you ten minutes _____, but your phone was busy.
11

Meg: That was my brother. He called me about 20 minutes _____. He
12

called me _____ evening too, but I was asleep.
13

Pamela: By the way, Mary Jane called me _____ Friday. She's getting
14

married!

Meg: Really! Who's the lucky man?

Pamela: His name is Tony Bradson. She started to work with him three years

_____ , and they decided to get married last year. So they saved
15

some money and decided on the wedding date _____ month.
16

Meg: Tony Bradson? Are you sure?

Pamela: Yes, why?

6 | What Do You Think?

Why is Meg surprised?

Example:
Meg knows Tony Bradson.

7 | Your Turn

A.
Talk about yourself with a partner. Use the time expressions.

Example:
Three months ago, I was in Rio de Janeiro.

1. Three months ago,
2. Last year,
3. Last night,
4. Yesterday morning,
5. One hour ago,

B.
Write five things that your partner told you.

Example:
Three months ago, she was in Seoul.

1. _____.
2. _____.
3. _____.
4. _____.
5. _____.

6c Spelling of Regular Past Tense Verbs

The baby cr**ied** and cr**ied.**
Then it look**ed** at me and stop**ped.**

Verb Ending	Spelling Rule	Examples	
1. Most regular verbs.	Add –*ed*.	rain point	rain**ed** point**ed**
2. Verb ends in *e*.	Add –*d*.	arrive smile	arriv**ed** smil**ed**
3. Verb ends in consonant + *y*.	Change *y* to *i* and add -*ed*.	try carry	tr**ied** carr**ied**
4. Verb ends in vowel + *y*.	Add –*ed*.	enjoy play	enjoy**ed** play**ed**
5. Verb ends in one consonant + vowel + consonant (one-syllable verbs).	Double the consonant and add –*ed*.	stop rub	stop**ped** rub**bed**
6. Verb ends in *x, w*.	Add -*ed*.	show fix	show**ed** fix**ed**
7. Verb ends in vowel + consonant and stress is on the first syllable (two-syllable verb).	Add –*ed*. Do not double the consonant.	visit answer	visit**ed** answer**ed**
8. Verb ends in vowel + consonant and stress is on the second syllable (two-syllable verb).	Double the consonant and add –*ed*.	prefer occur	prefer**red** occur**red**

Write the correct spelling of the simple past tense form.

Base Verb	Past Tense Verb	Base Verb	Past Tense Verb
1. add	*added*	11. stop	_____
2. carry	_____	12. hurry	_____
3. allow	_____	13. wait	_____
4. show	_____	14. stay	_____
5. count	_____	15. cry	_____
6. erase	_____	16. drop	_____
7. fit	_____	17. study	_____
8. marry	_____	18. taste	_____
9. die	_____	19. cook	_____
10. fail	_____	20. worry	_____

9 Practice

Work with a partner. Read the verbs from one list. Your partner writes the simple past tense. Then your partner reads the verbs from the other list and you write the simple past tense. Share your answers.

List A		List B	
1. listen	*listened*	1. start	_____
2. mix	_____	2. study	_____
3. smile	_____	3. fix	_____
4. kiss	_____	4. refer	_____
5. pick	_____	5. hug	_____
6. shop	_____	6. touch	_____
7. tip	_____	7. live	_____
8. reply	_____	8. clap	_____
9. open	_____	9. enter	_____
10. permit	_____	10. occur	_____
11. happen	_____	11. offer	_____
12. prefer	_____	12. admit	_____

10 Practice

Now write the past tense verbs from Exercise 9 in the correct column.

Add -ed	Add -d	Change y to i and add -ed	Double the consonant and add -ed
listened	smiled	studied	hugged

11 Practice

Look at the postcard and complete the sentences. Use the simple past of the verbs from the list.

arrive	climb	enjoy	prefer	shop	walk
carry	decide	enter	rain	visit	watch

Dear Mom and Dad,

Greetings from New York! We __arrived__ last
                                    1
Friday. It _____ all weekend, so we
                    2
_____ umbrellas. We _____ in the
        3   4
big stores on Fifth Avenue, but I _____ the
                                        5
small shops in the East Village. We _____
                                            6
the Statue of Liberty. We _____ at her feet
                                7
and _____ up to her head. That was great!
        8
We _____ around Central Park and
        9
Chinatown and even _____ a parade in the
                            10
streets. Last night, we _____ to go to Little
                                11
Italy to have dinner. The food was delicious and we
_____ the lovely Italian music.
        12

See you soon!
Susan

Mr. and Mrs. Bronson
1925 Franklin Avenue
Los Angeles, CA 90027

12 Your Turn

Write a postcard to a friend telling him or her about a place you visited. Use the verbs from the list or use your own. Use the simple past tense.

camp	hike	shop	swim	watch
climb	plan	ski	try	waterski
go boating	read	snow	visit	

Dear _____,

Greetings from _____

_____

_____

_____

_____

_____

_____

_____

See you soon!

_____

_____

_____

Practice

Complete the sentences with the verbs in parentheses. Use the present progressive, simple present, or simple past.

Jennifer: Hello Brad. It's Jennifer. How (be) _____*are*_____ you?
                                                            1

Brad: I (be) _____ fine, Jennifer. I (arrive) _____ in Hawaii
                          2   3
          yesterday morning and right now I (walk) _____ on the beach,
                                                              4
          and I (talk)_____ to you.
                          5

Jennifer: It (sound) _____ wonderful! (think) _____ you _____
                            6   7   8
          about me?

Brad: Of course, I (think) _____ about all the work you have in the
                                          9
          office.

Jennifer: Yes, I (have) _____ so much work. By the way, Tommy Jones
                              10
          (call) _____ you at the office yesterday. He
                      11
          (ask) _____ about you and (want) _____
                      12   13
          to speak to you. I said you (be) _____ out of town.
                                                    14

Brad: Good.

Jennifer: By the way, where (stay) _____ you _____?
                                          15   16

Brad: I (stay) _____ at the Sands Hotel on Waikiki Beach. I
           17

           (have) _____ a beautiful room.
           18

Jennifer: (have) _____ it _____ a view?
           19   20

Brad: Yes, it (have) _____ a beautiful view of the ocean.
           21

Jennifer: How (be) _____ the meeting yesterday?
           22

Brad: The meeting (be) _____ fine. After the meeting we all
           23

           (walk) _____ to a restaurant on the beach. The waiter
           24

           (offer) _____ us a table under the stars and
           25

           (allow) _____ us to choose the music. And we
           26

           (dance) _____ all night. I really (enjoy) _____ it.
           27   28

Jennifer: Oh, really? You (dance) _____! Who with?
                                    29

14 What Do You Think?

What does Brad say next? Write the next two lines of their conversation in Practice 13.

Example:
Brad: Oh, just a woman from the meeting.
Jennifer: Was she a good dancer?

15 Your Turn

Write a sentence about yourself in the simple past tense with each of these verbs.

1. visit   *I visited my grandparents last summer.*
            _____

2. prefer   _____
            _____

3. admit   _____
            _____

4. answer   _____
            _____

6d Pronunciation of -ed: /t/, /d/, and /id/

Elizabeth graduat**ed** last summer. I want**ed** to take her picture, so she smil**ed** and I photograph**ed** her with some of her friends.

Verb Ending	Pronunciation	Examples
1. Verb ends in voiceless *p, k, f, s, sh, ch.*	/t/	helped washed cooked
2. Verb ends in voiced *b, g, v, z, zh, th, j, m, n, ng, l, r,* or a vowel sound.	/d/	played lived rained
3. Verb ends in *d* or *t.*	/id/	waited wanted needed

16 Practice

Complete the sentences with the simple past tense of the verbs. Then read the sentences aloud and check the box for the pronunciation of each verb.

	/t/	/d/	/id/
Luis (open) __*opened*__ his eyes.		✓	
The hands on the clock (point) _____ to			
9:20. He (yawn) _____ and			
(stay) _____ in bed until 10:30.			

	/t/	/d/	/id/
Then he (shower) _____ ₅ and	_____	_____	_____
(shave) _____ ₆ .	_____	_____	_____
He (dress) _____ ₇ at 12:00 and	_____	_____	_____
(finish) _____ ₈ at around 1:00.	_____	_____	_____
Then he (walk) _____ ₉ to the café on the	_____	_____	_____
corner and (order) _____ ₁₀ breakfast.	_____	_____	_____
He (enjoy) _____ ₁₁ it as usual.	_____	_____	_____
It (start) _____ ₁₂ to rain, so	_____	_____	_____
he (call) _____ ₁₃ his friend and	_____	_____	_____
(invite) _____ ₁₄ him to his apartment	_____	_____	_____
to watch videos.	_____	_____	_____
His friend (arrive) _____ ₁₅ at 6:00 P.M. and	_____	_____	_____
they (watch) _____ ₁₆ videos and they	_____	_____	_____
(laugh) _____ ₁₇ a lot.	_____	_____	_____
At 10:00 P.M. the rain (stop) _____ ₁₈	_____	_____	_____
and his friend (want) _____ ₁₉ to go	_____	_____	_____
back home. It was now 11:00 P.M., and Luis			
(return) _____ ₂₀ to his favorite place—his bed!	_____	_____	_____

⎡17⎤ Practice

Complete the sentences with the simple past tense of the verbs from the list. Then circle the final *-ed* sound: /t/, /d/, or /id/.

answer	dry	need	shop	turn on	watch
cook	fold	play	talk	wash	

At 8:30 A.M. yesterday, Ann _____*played*_____ (t /(d)/ id) tennis with a friend.
₁

At 10:00, she _____ (t / d / id) her clothes. Then she
₂

_____ (t / d / id) her clothes in the dryer and
₃

_____ (t / d / id) them. At 12:00, she _____ (t / d / id)
₄   ₅

lunch. After lunch, she _____ (t / d / id) her computer and
_____ (t / d / id) her e-mail. Then she _____ (t / d / id)
                7   8
on the telephone with her friends. She _____ (t / d / id) to buy a
                                                        9
birthday gift for a friend. So she _____ (t / d / id) in the stores for a gift.
                                          10
By 9:00 P.M. she was at home and tired, so she _____ (t / d / id)
                                                              11
television.

18	Your Turn

Talk about yesterday. Say two things that you did using each of the following verbs.

enjoy   finish   need

Example:
Yesterday, I finished Exercise 10 in my grammar book.

6e   The Simple Past Tense: Irregular Verbs

Form

She **went** to Africa last year.
She **saw** a chimpanzee there.

Many verbs do not use the -*ed* form. The past form of these verbs is irregular.

Subject	Past Form of Verb (to go)	
I		
You		
He/She/It	went	to Africa last year.
We		
They		

The following are some common irregular verbs. For more irregular verbs, see page 199.

Base Form	Past Form
be	was/were
become	became
begin	began
buy	bought
come	came
do	did
eat	ate
drink	drank
feel	felt
fly	flew
get	got
give	gave
go	went
have	had
hear	heard
make	made
meet	met
put	put
say	said
see	saw
sit	sat
sleep	slept
read*	read*
stand	stood
take	took
teach	taught
tell	told
think	thought

*The base form *read* rhymes with *need*. The past form *read* is pronounced like *red*.

19 Practice

Complete the sentences with the simple past tense of the regular and irregular verbs in parentheses.

A Trip to Paris

Last April, Pete and Paula (fly) _____*flew*_____ to Paris from New York. They
1

(find) _____ a small hotel in the center of town. The hotel
2

(be, not) _____ expensive, and it (be) _____ clean.
3   4

Every morning, they (eat) _____ French bread and
5

(drink) _____ strong French coffee. They (take) _____
6   7

the Metro all the time. They (hear) _____ people sing in the subway.
8

One day, they (make) _____ friends with a French person. They
9

(be) _____ lucky because he (speak) _____ English. He
10   11

(tell) _____ them all the interesting places to visit. He also
12

(teach) _____ them two French words, *bonjour* and *merci*. They
13

(take) _____ a trip on the river Seine, and they (see) _____
14   15

a lot of interesting places.

One day, they (go) _____ shopping. They (buy) _____ French
16   17

perfume for gifts. Then they (sit) _____ outside in a café and
18

(have) _____ an expensive lunch. They (spend) _____ a lot of
19   20

money that day. Pete and Paula (think) _____ Paris was a very romantic city.
21

20 Practice

Complete the life story of Jane Goodall. Write the correct form of the verb in parentheses. Use the simple present, the present progressive, or the simple past.

Jane Goodall was born in London, England, in 1934. As a child she (love) _____*loved*_____

[1]

stories about Africa. She (finish) _____ school and (work) _____

[2]   [3]

for a film company. One day, a friend (invite) _____ her to Kenya, in Africa. She

[4]

(save) _____ money for the trip, and she (go) _____ there. Jane

[5]   [6]

(be) _____ 23 years old.

[7]

   In Kenya, she (meet) _____ Louis Leakey. He (be) _____ a

[8]   [9]

famous anthropologist (a person who studies humans and where they come from). Jane Goodall

(become) _____ his assistant. She (travel) _____ with Louis

[10]   [11]

Leakey and his wife in Africa.

   In 1960, she (begin) _____ to study chimpanzees. She

[12]

(live) _____ alone in the forest in Africa. Every morning,

[13]

she (go) _____ to the same place in the forest. The chimpanzees

[14]

(see) _____ her, but they (stand) _____ far away. After about six

[15]   [16]

months, the chimpanzees (come) _____ near her. Jane Goodall

[17]

(begin) _____ to know each chimpanzee. She (give) _____ each

[18]   [19]

chimpanzee a name. After years of work, she (discover) _____ many things about
                                                                    20
the chimpanzees. For example, chimpanzees (eat) _____ meat.
                                                                    21
        Today, the number of chimpanzees is not so great. People (kill) _____ the
                                                                                    22
chimpanzees or (cut) _____ down the forests where they live. Jane
                            23
(study) _____ chimpanzees for over 40 years. Now she
            24
(travel) _____ around the world and (talk) _____ about how
            25   26
to save the chimpanzees.

21 Practice

**Use the simple present or the simple past to complete the sentences about the story.
Use the verbs from the list.**

become	come	hear	talk
begin	go	live	travel

1. Today, Jane Goodall _____*travels*_____ all over the world.

2. In her lectures, she usually _____ about how to save the chimpanzees.

3. I _____ her speak in New York last year.

4. Ms. Goodall and a friend first _____ to Kenya over 40 years ago.

5. In 1960, she _____ to study chimpanzees in Africa.

6. She _____ in the forests of Africa to study the chimpanzees.

7. After about six months, the chimpanzees _____ near her.

8. Jane Goodall _____ an expert on chimpanzees.

22 Your Turn

**Tell your partner or your classmates about your life (or another person's life).
Use regular or irregular verbs from the list or use your own.**

arrive	give	pass my exams	stay
be	go	play	study
come	have	see	visit
finish	live	start	work

Example:
I was born in Cairo. My family lived in an apartment in the city.

6f   The Simple Past Tense: Negative

She **didn't have**
a dishwasher in 1940.

Subject	*Did Not*	Base Verb	
I			
You			
He/She/It	**did not**		
We	**didn't**	**have**	a dishwasher.
You			
They			

We use the base verb of the verb with *did not*.

CORRECT: He **did not walk.**
INCORRECT: He did not walked.

Practice

Look at the photo of people in 1948. First say what people did and didn't do in 1948. Use affirmative and negative simple past statements. Then write your sentences on the lines.

1. Children/wear/jeans _Children didn't wear jeans_ _____.

2. People/watch/television _____.

3. Many mothers/stay/at home _____.

4. Many mothers/work/outside _____.

5. People/eat/fast food _____.

6. Homes/have/computers _____.

7. Children/play/video games _____.

8. People/use/microwaves _____.

9. People/drink/a lot of soda _____.

10. Mothers/read/books to their children _____.

24 What Do You Think?

Say two things people did and two things people didn't do in the 1940s. Was life good or bad then? Say why.

Example:
Women didn't wear jeans. Women wore dresses. Life was not good because...

25 Practice

Monica is nice to Paul, but he isn't nice to her. Give the past tense of the verb in parentheses. Then complete the sentences with the negative form.

1. Monica (say) ___said___ hello to Paul today, but he ___didn't say hello to her___.

2. Monica (ask) _____ Paul, "How are you?", but _____.

3. Monica (call) _____ Paul yesterday, but _____.

4. Monica (write) _____ Paul a postcard, but _____.

5. Monica (give) _____ Paul a gift, but _____.

6. Monica (go) _____ to see Paul, but _____.

7. Monica (smile) _____ at Paul, but _____.

8. Monica (wait) _____ for Paul last week, but _____.

9. Monica (kiss) _____ Paul last week, but _____.

10. Monica (invite) _____ Paul to have lunch, but _____.

26 Your Turn

Say which of these activities you *did* or *didn't* do yesterday.

Example:
I didn't write a letter yesterday.
I made a phone call.

cook a meal	play a sport	visit a museum
go to the library	read a paper	walk for 20 minutes
listen to music	speak English	watch television
make a phone call	take a shower	write a letter

27 True or False Quiz

Work in groups or teams. Write and discuss six statements. Some should be true and some should not be true. Then ask a person from the other team if the statements are true or false. If a statement is false, the student must make the statement negative.

Example:
Statement: Edison invented the telephone.
Answer: False. Edison didn't invent the telephone.
Statement: It snowed last January in this city.
Answer: True.

The Simple Past Tense

6g The Simple Past Tense: Yes/No Questions

Doris: **Did you** turn off the gas? Albert: **Yes, I did.**

QUESTIONS			SHORT ANSWERS	
Did	Subject	Base Verb	Affirmative	Negative
Did	I you he she it we they	**work**	yesterday?	**Yes,** you **did.** I/we **did.** he **did.** she **did.** it **did.** you **did.** they **did.**	**No,** you **didn't.** I/we **didn't.** he **didn't.** she **didn't.** it **didn't.** you **didn't.** they **didn't.**

Complete the dialogue using the simple past tense of the words in parentheses.

Billy: (enjoy) _Did_ you _enjoy_ your vacation, Dolores?
                    1   2

Dolores: No, I _____ _didn't_ _____.
                         3

Billy: Why not?

Dolores: Well, I (not, like) _____ the food.
                                        4

Billy: (like) _____ you _____ the city?
                        5   6

Dolores: No, I _____.
                         7

Billy: What about the weather? (like) _____ you _____ it?
                                                  8   9

Dolores: No, I _____. It (rain) _____ every day.
                        10   11

Billy: (be) _____ the hotel good?
                        12

Dolores: No, it _____. Every time I (call) _____
                        13   14
            the reception desk, nobody (answer) _____.
                                                        15

Billy: (visit) _____ you _____ any museums?
                        16   17

Dolores: No, I _____. They (be) _____ all closed. It
                        18   19
            (be) _____ a holiday.
                        20

Billy: That's terrible. (go) _____ you _____ shopping at least?
                                        21   22

Dolores: Yes, I _____, but I (not, buy) _____ anything. It
                        23   24
            (be) _____ very expensive.
                        25

Billy: Well, (have) _____ you _____ a good flight?
                              26   27

Dolores: No, I _____. The flight (be) _____ five hours
                        28   29
            late, and the service (be) _____ terrible.
                                              30

Billy: So it (not, be) _____ a good vacation, I guess.
                                  31

Dolores: No, it (be) _____ NOT!
                              32

Practice

Julia, Ellen and Susan share an apartment. Julia left Ellen and Susan a list of things to do. She is talking on the phone to Ellen now. Complete the dialogue with simple past tense questions and affirmative and negative short answers.

check	eat	pay	wash
do	get	take out	water

Julia: Hello Ellen.

Ellen: Hi Julia.

Julia: Did you and Susan do the things I wrote on the list?

Ellen: Well, we did some of them.

Julia: Well, __*did*__ you __*check*__ the mail yesterday?
                1   2

Ellen: Yes, I _____, but I _____ the bills. I forgot.
               3   4

Julia: Uh-oh. _____ you _____ the food in the refrigerator?
             5   6

Ellen: No, I _____, but Susan _____. We didn't have time
             7   8
to go to the supermarket, so we just went to the small grocery store on the

corner, and we _____ bread and fresh milk.
                9

Julia: _____ Susan _____ the garbage?
       10   11

Ellen: _____, but she _____ the plants.
        12   13

Julia: _____ she _____ the dishes?
      14   15

Ellen: _____.
        16

Julia: One more thing, _____ you _____ the laundry?
                   17   18

Ellen: _____. I really didn't have time.
        19

Julia: That's OK. Thanks Ellen. See you tomorrow!

[30] Your Turn

Think of three questions to ask your partner about his/her last vacation/trip. Your partner will give a short answer, then give a long answer to explain.

Example:
You: Did you stay in a hotel?
Your partner: No, I didn't. I stayed in a guesthouse.

31 **Guess the Famous Person Quiz**

Work in groups. One person in the group thinks of a famous person from the past. The others in the group ask 20 yes/no questions to guess who the person is.

Example:
Was this person a man?   Yes./No.
Did he/she live in the USA?   Yes./No.

6h   The Simple Past Tense: Wh- Questions

Form

Brad: **Where** did you **go** on Sunday?
Dan: I went to the beach.
Brad: **What** did you **do**?
Dan: I went surfing, of course.

Wh-Question Base Verb	*Did*	Subject	Word
What		I	**talk** about?
When		you	**go** to the beach?
What time		he	**get** there?
Where	**did**	she	**stay?**
Who*		you	**call?**
How		we	**know** the place?
Why		they	**stay** at the beach all day?

Wh- Word as Subject		Past Tense Verb	
What		**happened?**	
Who		**called?**	

* In formal written English, the wh- word would be *whom*.

This is a photo of Steve's grandmother. Janine is asking Steve questions about his grandmother. Match the questions to the answers.

_____h_____ 1. How many children did she have?

_____ 2. When did she die?

_____ 3. How did she meet your grandfather?

_____ 4. Why did she want to go to Hollywood?

_____ 5. Where did she go in 1938?

_____ 6. Where did she grow up?

_____ 7. Who did she go to Hollywood with?

_____ 8. What did your grandfather do?

_____ 9. What happened to her parents?

a. They stayed in New York.

b. Because she wanted to be an actress.

c. He was an actor.

d. They were on the same train to California.

e. In 1998.

f. She went alone.

g. In Chicago.

h. Six.

i. To Hollywood.

33 **Practice**

Look at the pictures and write questions for the answers. Use the underlined words to help you choose the correct question word.

1. *Who did you see?*

   I saw <u>Karen</u>.

2. _____?

   I saw her <u>yesterday morning</u>.

3. _____?

   I saw her <u>in a café</u>.

4. _____?

   She looked <u>happy</u>.

5. _____?

   She found <u>an apartment</u>.

6. _____?

   She looked <u>in the newspaper</u>.

Items 1-6

7. _____?

   <u>Dave</u> had a bad day yesterday.

8. _____?

   He came home <u>at 10 P.M.</u>

9. _____?

   He felt <u>tired</u>.

10. _____?

    <u>Because he had a lot of work</u> to do.

Items 7-10

11. _____?

    I saw <u>Tina</u> yesterday.

12. _____?

    She was <u>in the street</u>.

13. _____?

    I saw her <u>in the afternoon</u>.

14. _____?

    She looked <u>happy</u>.

15. _____?

    She said <u>hello</u>.

Items 11-15

Read the story. Then write answers to the questions.

The Farmer and His Sons

Once there was an old farmer. The farmer was dying. Before he died, he wanted to teach his three sons how to be good farmers. He called his sons to him and said, "Boys, before I die I want you to know that there is a lot of money and gold buried in the vineyard. Promise me that you will look for it when I am dead." The sons promised to look for the money. After their father died, they started to look for the money. Every day they worked in the hot sun. They thought about the money all the time and worked hard to find it. They worked and worked but found nothing. They were very upset. But then the grapes started to grow on the vines. The grapes were the biggest and the best grapes in the neighborhood. The brothers sold the grapes and had a lot of money. Now they understood and lived happily until the end of their lives.

1. How many sons did the farmer have?

He had three sons .

2. Who did the farmer call?

_____ .

3. What did the sons promise?

_____.

4. When did they start to look for the money?

_____.

5. What did they find?

_____.

6. How did they feel?

_____.

7. What started to grow on the vines?

_____.

8. What did they do with the grapes?

_____.

9. What did they have in the end?

_____.

---

35 **Your Turn**

Work with a partner. Ask each other wh- questions about yesterday. Then tell the class about your partner's day.

Example:
You:	What time did you get up?
Your partner:	At 8:00.
You:	What did you have for breakfast?
Your partner:	Toast and tea.
You:	Where did you go after class?
Your partner:	To the cafe.

---

36 **Your Turn**

Work with a partner. Ask and answer questions about when you were children. Ask as many questions as you can. Write the answers. Then tell the class about your partner.

Example:
Where did you go to school?
Did you walk to school?
Did you like school?

6i The Simple Past Tense: Time Clauses with *Before* and *After*

I looked at my watch
before I called.

Main Clause	Time Clause
I looked at my watch	**before I called.**
She went home	**after she finished.**

Time Clause	Main Clause
Before I had dinner,	I went for a walk.
After we ate,	we watched television.

1. A time clause begins with a conjunction such as *before* or *after*.

2. A time clause has a subject and a verb, but it is not a complete sentence.

3. A time clause must be used with a main clause to form a complete sentence.

4. A time clause can come before or after a main clause. The meaning is the same. If the time clause comes first, it has a comma after it.

Underline the time clauses in the sentences. Circle the main clauses. Then rewrite the
sentence and change the order of the clauses.

1. After she got up, she brushed her teeth.

   She brushed her teeth after she got up .

2. She took a shower before she had breakfast.

   _____ .

3. She got dressed after she had breakfast.

   _____ .

4. Before she locked the door, she turned off the lights.

   _____ .

5. After she arrived at the office, she answered the phone.

   _____ .

6. She finished her day's work before she left the office.

   _____ .

7. She cooked dinner after she got home.

   _____ .

8. After she ate dinner, she washed the dishes.

   _____ .

9. She watched television before she went to bed.

   _____ .

10. Before she went to sleep, she read a book.

   _____ .

38 Practice

Combine the two sentences about the photos. Write one sentence with *after* and another with *before*. Then work with a partner to check the punctuation.

Example:

1. They got married. They had a baby.

   After they got married, they

   had a baby.

   Before they had a baby, they

   got married.

2. He learned to walk. He rode a bicycle.

   _____

   _____

   _____

   _____

3. He graduated from college. He worked for a company.

   _____

   _____

   _____

   _____

4. He became the president of the company. He... (Use your own idea.)

   _____

   _____

   _____

   _____

Write ten things you did before you came to class today. Use the phrases in the list or use your own.

do my homework	lock my door	take the bus/train
have breakfast	put my books in my bag	talk to my classmates
listen to the news	take a shower	

Example:

I had breakfast before I came to class today.

1. _____.

2. _____.

3. _____.

4. _____.

5. _____.

6. _____.

7. _____.

8. _____.

9. _____.

10. _____.

Write a narrative paragraph.

Step 1. Work with a partner. Find out about your partner's last vacation. Ask questions like these. Write the answers to the questions.

1. Where did you go?
2. When did you go?
3. Who/with?
4. How/get there?
5. Where/stay?
6. How long/stay?
7. How/hotel?

8. How/food?
9. How/people?
10. How/weather?
11. Did you spend a lot of money?
12. What/buy?
13. Did you have a good time?
14. Did you have any problems?

Step 2: Rewrite your answers in paragraph form. For more writing guidelines, see pages 202-207.

Step 3: Write a title in three or four words, for example, "My Last Vacation." Center the title above your paragraph.

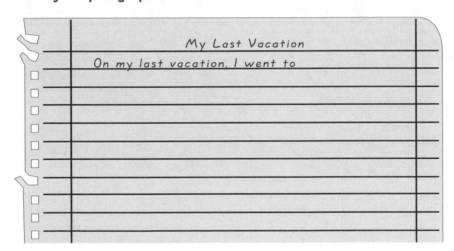

Step 4. Evaluate your paragraph.
Checklist
_____ Did you indent the first line?
_____ Did you give your paragraph a title?
_____ Did you put the title in the center, above your paragraph?
_____ Did you capitalize the title correctly? (See page 203.)

Step 5. Edit your work. Work with a partner to edit your sentences. Correct spelling, punctuation, vocabulary, and grammar.

Step 6. Write your final copy.

A **Choose the best answer, A, B, C, or D, to complete the sentence. Mark your answer by darkening the oval with the same letter.**

1. Who _____ to on the phone?

    A. you talk ⒶⒷⒸⒹ
    B. talked you
    C. did you talk
    D. did talk you

2. When I asked Richard a question, he _____ me.

    A. didn't answered ⒶⒷⒸⒹ
    B. didn't answer
    C. not answered
    D. no answered

3. When _____ home yesterday?

    A. you come ⒶⒷⒸⒹ
    B. come you
    C. did you come
    D. you come

4. Before I _____ to class yesterday, I studied for the test.

    A. came ⒶⒷⒸⒹ
    B. did come
    C. cames
    D. come

5. What _____?

    A. he did said ⒶⒷⒸⒹ
    B. did he said
    C. he said
    D. did he say

6. We went to a movie _____.

    A. yesterday night ⒶⒷⒸⒹ
    B. last yesterday
    C. last night
    D. night yesterday

7. Why _____ famous?

    A. did Lindberg become ⒶⒷⒸⒹ
    B. Lindberg he became
    C. did Lindberg became
    D. Lindberg became

8. Mozart _____ music when he was a child.

    A. write ⒶⒷⒸⒹ
    B. wrote
    C. did write
    D. writed

9. Thomas Edison _____ the airplane.

    A. didn't invent ⒶⒷⒸⒹ
    B. not invented
    C. not invent
    D. didn't invented

10. Where _____ yesterday afternoon?

    A. you went ⒶⒷⒸⒹ
    B. did you go
    C. did you went
    D. you did go

B Find the underlined word or phrase, A, B, C, or D, that is incorrect. Mark your answer by darkening the oval with the same letter.

1. Plato <u>was</u> a Greek philosopher who <u>lived</u>
        A   B

   and <u>died</u> more than two thousand years
       C

   <u>before</u>.
    D

   (A) (B) (C) (D)

2. <u>In</u> 1897, Boston <u>puts</u> streetcars
    A   B

   underground, <u>and</u> <u>completed</u> the first
               C   D

   American subway.

   (A) (B) (C) (D)

3. Webster's *American Spelling Book*, which

   he <u>wroted</u> in 1783, <u>sold</u> over 100 million
      A   B

   copies and <u>became</u> <u>a</u> best-selling book.
            C   D

   (A) (B) (C) (D)

4. Coffee <u>came from</u> Ethiopia and <u>was</u> a
         A   B

   popular drink in the Arab world before <u>it</u>
                             C

   <u>comes</u> to Europe.
    D

   (A) (B) (C) (D)

5. <u>How long</u> <u>ago</u> <u>did</u> the Egyptians <u>built</u>
      A   B   C   D

   the pyramids?

   (A) (B) (C) (D)

6. Helen Keller <u>was born</u> in 1889 and
              A

   <u>becomes</u> deaf and blind at the age of
     B

   twenty <u>months</u> after she <u>had</u> a fever.
          C   D

   (A) (B) (C) (D)

7. Peter the Great <u>tried</u> to modernize Russia
             A

   and <u>its</u> old <u>customs</u>, and he also <u>moves</u>
       B   C   D

   the capital from Moscow to St. Petersburg.

   (A) (B) (C) (D)

8. <u>When</u> Marco Polo and his father <u>returned</u>
    A   B

   to Italy from China in the 1200s,

   <u>they</u> <u>bring</u> with them ways to make
    C   D

   noodles.

   (A) (B) (C) (D)

9. <u>How long</u> <u>it take</u> to travel across
     A   B

   <u>the Atlantic Ocean</u> by ship two hundred
           C

   years <u>ago</u>?
        D

   (A) (B) (C) (D)

10. The Wright Brothers <u>invented</u> the airplane,
                     A

    <u>but</u> <u>they</u> <u>not invent</u> the telephone.
     B   C   D

    (A) (B) (C) (D)

UNIT 7

THE PAST PROGRESSIVE TENSE

7a The Past Progressive Tense

A: **What were** the women **doing** at 10:00 yesterday morning?

B: They **were working**, of course!

AFFIRMATIVE AND NEGATIVE STATEMENTS		
Subject	Past of *Be* (+ *Not*)	Base Verb + *-ing*
I	was was not wasn't	working.
You	were were not weren't	
He/She/It	was was not wasn't	
We They	were were not weren't	

YES/NO QUESTIONS			SHORT ANSWERS	
Past of *Be*	Subject	Base Verb + *-ing*	Affirmative	Negative
			Yes,	**No,**
Was	I		you **were.**	you **weren't.**
Were	you		I **was.**	I **wasn't.**
Was	he/she/it	**working?**	he **was.** she **was.** it **was.**	he **wasn't.** she **wasn't.** it **wasn't.**
Were	we you they		you **were.** we **were.** they **were.**	you **weren't.** we **weren't.** they **weren't.**

WH- QUESTIONS			
Wh- Word	Past of *Be*	Subject	Verb + *ing*
What	**was**	I	**saying?**
Where	**were**	you	**going?**
When	**was**	he/she/it	**working?**
Why	**were**	you	**running?**
Who*	**were**	they	**watching?**

* In formal written English, the wh- word would be *whom*.

Tony **was sleeping** at 10:00 yesterday.

We use the past progressive for an action that was already happening at a particular time in the past.

Tony **was sleeping** at 10:00 yesterday. (He started to sleep before 10:00. He was still sleeping at 10:00 yesterday.)

Practice

What was happening in the neighborhood on Sunday at 11:00 in the morning? Look at the photos. Ask and answer questions using the prompts. Work in pairs.

1. Dad/wash/his car

A: _What was Dad doing?_

B: _He was washing_

his car.

2. Karen/play/the violin

A: _____

_____

B: _____

_____

3. Bob/get/dressed

A: _____

_____

B: _____

_____

4. Nancy/talk/on the phone

A: _____

_____

B: _____

_____

5. Mike/drive/his car

A: _____

_____

B: _____

_____

6. the cat/watch/the birds

A: _____

_____

B: _____

_____

7. Tim/work/on his computer

A: _____

_____

B: _____

_____

8. Eric and Sherry/jog

A: _____

_____

B: _____

_____

9. Laurie/swim

A: _____

_____

B: _____

_____

10. Ben/shop/at the market

A: _____

_____

B: _____

_____

11. Julio/garden

A: _____

_____

B: _____

_____

12. Cheryl and Benny/make cookies

A: _____

_____

B: _____

_____

---

2 Practice

Work with a partner. Ask and answer the questions.

Example:

at seven o'clock yesterday evening

You: What were you doing at seven o'clock yesterday evening?

Your partner: I was eating dinner.

1. at 12:00 noon on Sunday

2. at midnight last night

3. at seven this morning

4. an hour ago

5. at this time yesterday

6. five minutes ago

Practice

Answer the questions with a negative past progressive verb. Then add a statement with the cue in parentheses.

1. Was Sue doing her homework when I called?

   No, _she wasn't doing her homework_____.

   (clean her apartment) _She was cleaning her apartment_____.

2. Were Dave and Bob talking about the basketball game?

   No, _____.

   (talk about the soccer game) _____.

3. Were you trying to reach me?

   No, _____.

   (try to reach your brother) _____.

4. Was I speaking too loudly?

   No, _____.

   (speak too softly) _____.

5. Were you reading the New York Times?

   No, _____.

   (read the Los Angeles Times) _____.

6. Was the teacher explaining the present progressive tense?

   No, _____.

   (explain the past progressive tense) _____.

7b *While* and *When* with Past Time Clauses

While he was driving,
a man crossed the street.

1. *While* can begin a time clause.
2. The verb in a *while* clause is often in the past progressive tense.

WHILE	
Main Clause	Time Clause
A man crossed the street	**while he was driving.**
Time Clause	Main Clause
While he was driving,	a man crossed the street.

3. *When* can begin a time clause.
4. The verb in a *when* clause is often in the simple past tense.

WHEN	
Main Clause	Time Clause
Jenny was working at the office	**when Tony called.**
Time Clause	Main Clause
When Tony called,	Jenny was working at the office

RULES FOR TIME CLAUSES

5. A time clause can go at the beginning or at the end of a sentence. If it is at the beginning, we use a comma after it.

6. A time clause alone is not a complete sentence. We must use it with a main clause to form a complete sentence.

COMPLETE SENTENCE: When Tony called, Jenny was working at the office.

INCOMPLETE SENTENCE: ~~When Tony called.~~

4 Practice

Tony and Linda had a bad day yesterday. Find out what happened. Match the sentence parts.

A	B
_g_ **1.** Tony was sleeping when	**a.** he cut his chin.
_____ **2.** Linda was walking to the store when	**b.** it had a problem.
_____ **3.** Linda was waiting for the bus when	**c.** she burned her finger.
_____ **4.** Linda was standing in the rain when	**d.** the doorbell rang.
_____ **5.** Tony was driving to work when	**e.** the bus finally came.
_____ **6.** Tony was shaving when	**f.** she tripped and fell.
_____ **7.** Tony was taking a shower when	**g.** the telephone rang and woke him up.
_____ **8.** Tony was working on his computer when	**h.** he had an accident.
_____ **9.** Linda was cooking when	**i.** it started to rain and she got wet.

5 Practice

Complete the sentences with the simple past or the past progressive of the verbs in parentheses.

We (talk) _____were talking_____ about the questions on the test when the teacher
                    1
(walk) _____ into the classroom. While she (give) _____
              2   3
out the tests, we (sit) _____ in silence. It was 9:15. We started the test.
                            4
While we (take) _____ the test, the teacher (watch) _____
                      5   6
us. While Leo (take) _____ the test, he (talk) _____ to
                            7   8
himself. He (talk) _____ to himself when the teacher (tell) _____
                        9   10
him, "Be quiet, Leo." His face became red.

When the teacher (say) _____ "STOP! Pens down," many students
                            11
(write) _____. I (finish) _____ my last answer when
              12   13
the teacher (say) _____ "STOP." I (smile) _____ when
                      14   15
I (leave) _____ the classroom. While I (walk) _____
              16   17
home, I (say) _____ to myself, "I did a great job on that test."
                    18

7c   The Past Progressive Tense and The Simple Past Tense

Tense	Function	Examples
Past Progressive	We use the past progressive for an action that was already happening at a particular time in the past.	The students **were studying** English grammar at 10:15 yesterday morning. (They were studying *before* 10:15 and *at* 10:15.)
	We use the past progressive for an action that was happening when another action interrupted it.	She **was working** when Jim **called**. While Bob **was sleeping** last night, the telephone **rang**.
Simple Past	We use the simple past for an action that began and ended at a particular time in the past.	I **called** my mother last Sunday. She **arrived** at 9:30 yesterday. They **went** to Mexico in June last year.
	We use the simple past to show that one action immediately followed another action.	When I **opened** the door, I **saw** my sister. (First I opened the door. Then I saw my sister.)

6   Practice

Use the simple past or past progressive of the verbs in parentheses.

A.

One day I (study) ____was studying____ in the library when I (see) _____
1   2
her. She (come) _____ towards me and (sit) _____ down in the
3   4
chair next to me. Then she (put) _____ on her glasses and
5
(start) _____ to read a book. While she (read) _____ I
6   7
(look) _____ at her quickly for a moment. Suddenly our eyes
8
(meet) _____. I (smile) _____ and then she
9   10
(smile) _____.
11

B.

I had a bad dream last night. In my dream it was Sunday morning. It was ten o'clock
and I (read) _____ a book in the yard in front of the house. Suddenly the
1
sky (become) _____ dark. It (start) _____ to rain so I
2   3
(go) _____ inside the house. I (close) _____ the windows
4   5

and (turn) _____ on the television to listen to the news and weather. I
                    6
(watch) _____ the news when the storm (begin) _____.
              7   8
I remember that the wind (blow) _____ and the windows
                                         9
(shake) _____ when I (hear) _____ a terrible noise like a
              10   11
big bang. Then I (wake) _____ up on the floor.
                              12

C.

    It (get) _____ dark when I (get) _____ off the train.
                  1   2
There was no one in the street. While I (walk) _____ down the street,
                                                        3
I (hear) _____ footsteps behind me. When I
              4
(begin) _____ to walk fast, the footsteps (get) _____
              5   6
fast. When I (begin) _____ to run, the footsteps
                          7
(get) _____ faster. Finally, I (get) _____ to my house. I
            8   9
(shake) _____ when I (put) _____ the key in the door.
              10   11
Just then I (hear) _____ a man's voice behind me. "Is this your purse?
                          12
You left it on the train."

| 7 | Practice |

Look at the information about Mike and Lillian. Then complete the sentences about them using the past progressive or the simple past. Some verbs must be negative.

Mike		Lillian	
1994-2000	lived in Boston	March 12, 1996	arrived in New York
2000-2001	took computer course	1996-2004	lived in New York
2001-2002	lived and worked in Japan	1996-1999	studied at the university
2002-2005	worked for Microdisc	1998-2000	worked for a computer company
2002	met Lillian	2002	met Mike
2004	married Lillian	2004	married Mike

1. In 1994, Mike _____*was living*_____ in Boston.

2. When Lillian _____ in New York in 1996, Mike _____
   in Boston.

3. In 2000, Lillian _____ in New York.

4. From 1996 to 1999, Lillian _____ at a university in New York.

5. In 2001, Mike _____ in Japan, and he _____ there, too.

6. In 2002, Lillian _____ Mike.

7. Lillian _____ in New York when she _____ Mike.

8. In 1999, Lillian _____ for a computer company.

9. Mike _____ for Microdisc when he met Lillian.

10. Lillian married Mike while he _____ for Microdisc.

8 Practice

Look at the following results of different actions. What do you think the person was doing in each situation? Work with a partner and write an answer. Then compare your answers in groups.

1. He burned his finger.

   *Maybe he was cooking when he burned his finger*_____.

2. She started to cry.

   _____.

3. He fell down.

   _____.

4. It fell and broke to pieces.

   _____.

5. He fell asleep.

   _____.

6. We heard a strange noise.

   _____.

7. I saw a man's head in the window.

   _____.

8. The lights went out.

   _____.

9. She laughed loudly.

   _____.

9 Your Turn

Describe a bad day that you had to the class using *while* and *when*. What unexpected thing happened while you were doing something else?

Example:
I had a very bad day last week. I was watching television at home ...

WRITING: Narrate Events

Step 1. Write four important things that happened in your life and give the dates.

	Date	**What Happened**
Example:	1986-2003	lived in Mexico City, Mexico
	2004	started college

1. _____ _____
2. _____ _____
3. _____ _____
4. _____ _____

Step 2. Work with a partner. Ask and answer questions. Find out what your partner was doing at the time important things happened in your life. Write the answers to these questions.

Example:

A: What were you doing while I was living in Mexico from 1980 to 1999?
B: I was living in Seoul, Korea.

Step 3. Rewrite what happened to you and what your partner was doing using *when* and *while*. Write a title. For more writing guidelines, see pages 202-207.

Example:
Two Lives/My Life and (your partner's name) Life.

Two Lives

While I was living in Mexico City, Kim was living in Seoul.

Step 4. Evaluate your paragraph.
Checklist
_____ Did you indent the first line?
_____ Did you give your paragraph a title?
_____ Did you capitalize the title correctly?
_____ Did you use verb tenses correctly?

Step 5. Work with a partner to edit your paragraph. Correct spelling, punctuation, vocabulary, and grammar.

Step 6. Write your final copy.

A   Choose the best answer A, B, C, or D, to complete the sentence. Mark your answer by darkening the oval with the same letter.

1. It _____ here every winter.

    A. snows   Ⓐ Ⓑ Ⓒ Ⓓ
    B. was snowing
    C. is snowing
    D. snow

2. _____ now?

    A. It is raining   Ⓐ Ⓑ Ⓒ Ⓓ
    B. Is it raining
    C. Does it rain
    D. Is raining

3. At 11:00 yesterday morning, we _____ in this classroom.

    A. sat   Ⓐ Ⓑ Ⓒ Ⓓ
    B. sitting
    C. were sat
    D. were sitting

4. When she heard the news, she _____ to cry.

    A. was beginning   Ⓐ Ⓑ Ⓒ Ⓓ
    B. begin
    C. began
    D. begins

5. I saw Karen in a store yesterday, but she _____ me.

    A. does not see   Ⓐ Ⓑ Ⓒ Ⓓ
    B. did not see
    C. was not seeing
    D. not saw

6. I woke up when the alarm clock _____.

    A. rings   Ⓐ Ⓑ Ⓒ Ⓓ
    B. did ring
    C. was ringing
    D. rang

7. While I _____ to school, I met my friend.

    A. was walking   Ⓐ Ⓑ Ⓒ Ⓓ
    B. walked
    C. walk
    D. am walking

8. I _____ my room when I found my keys.

    A. am cleaning   Ⓐ Ⓑ Ⓒ Ⓓ
    B. cleaned
    C. clean
    D. was cleaning

9. _____ when you arrived?

    A. Were the children sleeping   Ⓐ Ⓑ Ⓒ Ⓓ
    B. The children slept
    C. Did the children sleep
    D. The children were sleeping

10. I'm sorry. I _____ time to call you yesterday.

    A. didn't have   Ⓐ Ⓑ Ⓒ Ⓓ
    B. wasn't having
    C. don't have
    D. wasn't have

B Find the underlined word or phrase, A, B, C, or D, that is incorrect. Mark your answer by darkening the oval with the same letter.

1. We <u>walking</u> <u>in the park</u> <u>when</u> the rain
   A   B   C

   <u>started</u>.
   D

   Ⓐ Ⓑ Ⓒ Ⓓ

2. <u>Buildings</u> <u>began</u> to shake <u>when</u> people
    A   B   C

   <u>were sleeping</u>.
   D

   Ⓐ Ⓑ Ⓒ Ⓓ

3. The Titanic <u>traveled</u> fast <u>when</u> <u>it</u> <u>hit</u> a
         A   B   D C

   huge iceberg in the sea.

   Ⓐ Ⓑ Ⓒ Ⓓ

4. <u>While</u> Mozart <u>was born</u>, <u>his father</u> <u>worked</u>
  A   B   C   D

   as a violinist at the court of Salzburg in
   Austria.

   Ⓐ Ⓑ Ⓒ Ⓓ

5. The explorer, Marco Polo, <u>was</u> in <u>a</u> prison
                   A   B

   <u>when</u> he <u>is writing</u> about his travels in
   C   D

   the East.

   Ⓐ Ⓑ Ⓒ Ⓓ

6. <u>When</u> Thomas Edison <u>was</u> <u>a child</u>, he
  A   B   C

   <u>wasn't liking</u> to go to school.
   D

   Ⓐ Ⓑ Ⓒ Ⓓ

7. <u>Last night</u>, my brother <u>was watching</u>
    A   B

   television and <u>eat</u> <u>chocolates</u> at the same
            C   D

   time.

   Ⓐ Ⓑ Ⓒ Ⓓ

8. <u>When</u> <u>was</u> the semester <u>begin</u>, on the 14th
  A   B   C

   <u>or</u> 15th of September?
   D

   Ⓐ Ⓑ Ⓒ Ⓓ

9. <u>When</u> I <u>was seeing</u> the <u>president's wife</u>,
  A   B   C

   she <u>was wearing</u> a red dress.
       D

   Ⓐ Ⓑ Ⓒ Ⓓ

10. <u>While</u> they <u>were traveling</u> across Europe
   A   B

   by car, they <u>were having</u> <u>an accident</u>.
            C   D

   Ⓐ Ⓑ Ⓒ Ⓓ

APPENDICES

Appendix 1   Grammar Terms

Adjective

An adjective describes a noun or a pronoun.

> My cat is very **intelligent**.
>
> He's **orange** and **white**.

Adverb

An adverb describes a verb, another adverb, or an adjective.

> Joey speaks **slowly**.
>
> Joey **always** visits his father on Wednesdays.
>
> His father cooks **extremely** well.
>
> His father is a **very** talented chef.

Article

An article comes before a noun. The definite article is *the*. The indefinite articles are *a* and *an*.

> I read **an** online story and **a** magazine feature about celebrity lifestyles.
>
> **The** online story was much more interesting than **the** magazine feature.

Auxiliary Verb

An auxiliary verb is found with a main verb. It is often called a "helping" verb.

> Susan **can't** play in the game this weekend.
>
> **Does** Ruth play baseball?
>
> Where **does** Ruth play baseball?

Base Form

The base form of a verb has no tense. It has no endings (*–ed, –s,* or *–ing*).

> Jill didn't **see** the band.
>
> She should **see** them the next time they are in town.

Comparative

Comparative forms compare two things. They can compare people, places, or things.

> This orange is **sweeter than** that grapefruit.
>
> Working in a large city is **more stressful than** working in a small town.

Conjunction

A conjunction joins two or more sentences, adjectives, nouns, or prepositional phrases. Some conjunctions are *and, but,* and *or.*

Kasey is efficient, **and** her work is excellent.

Her apartment is small **but** comfortable.

She works Wednesdays **and** Thursdays.

Contraction

A contraction is composed of two words put together with an apostrophe. Some letters are left out.

Frank usually **doesn't** answer his phone.   (doesn't = does + not)

He's really busy.   (he's = he + is)

Does he know what time **we're** meeting?   (we're = we + are)

Imperative

An imperative gives a command or directions. It uses the base form of the verb, and it does not use the word *you*.

Please **tell** me how to get there.

Go to the corner and **turn** left.

Modal

A modal is a type of auxiliary verb. The modal auxiliaries are *can, could, may, might, must, shall, should, will,* and *would*.

Elizabeth **will** act the lead role in the play next week.

She **couldn't** go to the party last night because she had to practice her lines.

She **may** be able to go to the party this weekend.

Noun

A noun is a person, an animal, a place, or a thing.

My **brother** and **sister-in-law** live in **Pennsylvania**.

They have three **cats**.

Their favorite sports are **skiing** and **cycling**.

Object

An object is the noun or pronoun that receives the action of the verb.

Georgie sent **a gift** for Johnny's birthday.

Johnny thanked **her** for the gift.

Preposition

A preposition is a small connecting word that is followed by a noun or pronoun. Some are a*t, above, after, by, before, below, for, in, of, off, on, over, to, under, up,* and *with*.

Every day, Jay drives Chris and Ally **to** school **in** the new car.

In the afternoon, he waits **for** them **at** the bus stop.

Pronoun

A pronoun takes the place of a noun.

Chris loves animals. **He** has two dogs and two cats.

His pets are very friendly. **They** like to spend time with people.

Sentence

A sentence is a group of words that has a subject and a verb. It is complete by itself.

Sentence: Brian works as a lawyer.

Not a sentence: Works as a lawyer.

Subject

A subject is the noun or pronoun that does the action in the sentence.

Trisha is from Canada.

She writes poetry about nature.

Superlative

Superlative forms compare three or more people, places, or things.

Jennifer is **the tallest** girl in the class.

She is from Paris, which is **the most romantic** city in the world.

Tense

Tense tells when the action in a sentence happens.

Simple present	–	The cat **eats** fish every morning.
Present progressive	–	He **is eating** fish now.
Simple past	–	He **ate** fish yesterday morning.
Past progressive	–	He **was eating** when the doorbell rang.
Future with *be going to*	–	He **is going to eat** fish tomorrow morning too!
Future with *will*	–	I think that he **will eat** the same thing next week.

Verb

A verb tells the action in a sentence.

Melissa **plays** guitar in a band.

She **loves** writing new songs.

The band **has** four other members.

Appendix 2 Numbers and Calendar Information

Numbers

Cardinal Numbers

1	=	one
2	=	two
3	=	three
4	=	four
5	=	five
6	=	six
7	=	seven
8	=	eight
9	=	nine
10	=	ten
11	=	eleven
12	=	twelve
13	=	thirteen
14	=	fourteen
15	=	fifteen
16	=	sixteen
17	=	seventeen
18	=	eighteen
19	=	nineteen
20	=	twenty
21	=	twenty-one
22	=	twenty-two
23	=	twenty-three
24	=	twenty-four
25	=	twenty-five
26	=	twenty-six
27	=	twenty-seven
28	=	twenty-eight
29	=	twenty-nine
30	=	thirty
40	=	forty
50	=	fifty

Ordinal Numbers

1st	=	first
2nd	=	second
3rd	=	third
4th	=	fourth
5th	=	fifth
6th	=	sixth
7th	=	seventh
8th	=	eighth
9th	=	ninth
10th	=	tenth
11th	=	eleventh
12th	=	twelfth
13th	=	thirteenth
14th	=	fourteenth
15th	=	fifteenth
16th	=	sixteenth
17th	=	seventeenth
18th	=	eighteenth
19th	=	nineteenth
20th	=	twentieth
21st	=	twenty-first
22nd	=	twenty-second
23rd	=	twenty-third
24th	=	twenty-fourth
25th	=	twenty-fifth
26th	=	twenty-sixth
27th	=	twenty-seventh
28th	=	twenty-eighth
29th	=	twenty-ninth
30th	=	thirtieth
40th	=	fortieth
50th	=	fiftieth

Cardinal Numbers

60	=	sixty
70	=	seventy
80	=	eighty
90	=	ninety
100	=	one hundred
200	=	two hundred
1,000	=	one thousand
10,000	=	ten thousand
100,000	=	one hundred thousand
1,000,000	=	one million

Ordinal Numbers

60th	=	sixtieth
70th	=	seventieth
80th	=	eightieth
90th	=	ninetieth
100th	=	one hundredth
200th	=	two hundredth
1,000th	=	one thousandth
10,000th	=	ten thousandth
100,000th	=	one hundred thousandth
1,000,000th	=	one millionth

Calendar Information

Days of the Week

	Abbreviation
Monday	Mon.
Tuesday	Tue.
Wednesday	Wed.
Thursday	Thurs.
Friday	Fri.
Saturday	Sat.
Sunday	Sun.

Months of the year

	Abbreviation
January	Jan.
February	Feb.
March	Mar.
April	Apr.
May	May
June	Jun.
July	Jul.
August	Aug.
September	Sept.
October	Oct.
November	Nov.
December	Dec.

Appendices

Appendix 3   Irregular Verbs

Base Form	Simple Past	Past Participle	Base Form	Simple Past	Past Participle
be	was, were	been	keep	kept	kept
become	became	become	know	knew	known
begin	began	begun	leave	left	left
bend	bent	bent	lend	lent	lent
bite	bit	bitten	lose	lost	lost
blow	blew	blown	make	made	made
break	broke	broken	meet	met	met
bring	brought	brought	pay	paid	paid
build	built	built	put	put	put
buy	bought	bought	read	read	read
catch	caught	caught	ride	rode	ridden
choose	chose	chosen	ring	rang	rung
come	came	come	run	ran	run
cost	cost	cost	say	said	said
cut	cut	cut	see	saw	seen
do	did	done	sell	sold	sold
draw	drew	drawn	send	sent	sent
drink	drank	drunk	shake	shook	shaken
drive	drove	driven	shut	shut	shut
eat	ate	eaten	sing	sang	sung
fall	fell	fallen	sit	sat	sat
feed	fed	fed	sleep	slept	slept
feel	felt	felt	speak	spoke	spoken
fight	fought	fought	spend	spent	spent
find	found	found	stand	stood	stood
fly	flew	flown	steal	stole	stolen
forget	forgot	forgotten	swim	swam	swum
get	got	gotten/got	take	took	taken
give	gave	given	teach	taught	taught
go	went	gone	tear	tore	torn
grow	grew	grown	tell	told	told
hang	hung	hung	think	thought	thought
have	had	had	throw	threw	thrown
hear	heard	heard	understand	understood	understood
hide	hid	hidden	wake up	woke up	woken up
hit	hit	hit	wear	wore	worn
hold	held	held	win	won	won
hurt	hurt	hurt	write	wrote	written

Appendix 4   Spelling Rules for Endings

Adding a Final –s to Nouns and Verbs

Rule	Example	–s
1. For most words, add –s without making any changes.	book bet save play	books bets saves plays
2. For words ending in a consonant + *y*, change the *y* to *i* and add –es.	study party	studies parties
3. For words ending in *ch, s, sh, x,* or *z,* add –es.	church class wash fix quiz	churches classes washes fixes quizzes
4. For words ending in *o,* sometimes add –es and sometimes add –s.	potato piano	potatoes pianos
5. For words ending in *f* or *lf,* change the *f* or *lf* to *v* and add –es. For words ending in *fe,* change the *f* to *v* and add –s.	loaf half life	loaves halves lives

Adding a Final *-ed*, *-er*, *-est*, and *-ing*

Rule	Example	*-ed*	*-er*	*-est*	*-ing*
1. For most words, add the ending without making any changes.	clean	cleaned	cleaner	cleanest	cleaning
2. For words ending in silent *e*, drop the *e* and add the ending.	save like nice	saved liked	saver nicer	 nicest	saving liking
3. For words ending in a consonant + *y*, change the *y* to *i* and add *-ed*, *-er*, or *-est*. Do not change or drop the *y* before adding *-ing*.	sunny happy study worry	 studied worried	sunnier happier	sunniest happiest	 studying worrying
4. For one-syllable words ending in one vowel and one consonant, double the final consonant, then add the ending. Do not double the last consonant if it is a *w, x,* or *y*.	hot run bat glow mix stay	 batted glowed mixed stayed	hotter runner batter mixer	hottest	 running batting glowing mixing staying
5. For words of two or more syllables that end in one vowel and one consonant, double the final consonant if the final syllable is stressed.	begin refer occur permit	 referred occurred permitted	beginner		beginning referring occurring permitting
6. For words of two or more syllables that end in one vowel and one consonant, do NOT double the final consonant if the final syllable is NOT stressed.	enter happen develop	entered happened developed	developer		entering happening developing

Appendix 5   Capitalization Rules

First words

1. Capitalize the first word of every sentence.

   They live in San Francisco.   **W**hat is her name?

2. Capitalize the first word of a quotation.

   She said, "**M**y name is Nancy."

Names

1. Capitalize names of people, including titles of address.

   Mr. **T**hompson   **A**lison **E**mmet   **M**ike **A**. **L**ee

2. Capitalize the word "I".

   Rose and **I** went to the market.

3. Capitalize nationalities, ethnic groups, and religions.

   Korean   **L**atino   **A**sian   **I**slam

4. Capitalize family words if they appear alone or with a name, but not if they have a possessive pronoun or article.

   Where's **D**ad?   vs.   Where's my **f**ather?

   He's at **A**unt Lucy's house.   vs.   He's at an **a**unt's house.

Places

1. Capitalize the names of countries, states, cities, and geographical areas.

   Mexico   **V**irginia   **T**okyo   the **S**outh

2. Capitalize the names of oceans, lakes, rivers, and mountains.

   the **P**acific **O**cean **L**ake **O**ntario   the **N**ile   **M**t. **E**verest

3. Capitalize the names of streets, schools, parks, and buildings.

   Main **S**treet   **C**entral **P**ark

   the **U**niversity of **C**alifornia   the **E**mpire **S**tate **B**uilding

4. Don't capitalize directions if they aren't names of geographical areas.

   She lives **n**ortheast of Washington.   We fly **s**outh during our flight.

Time words

1. Capitalize the names of days and months.

    Monday   **F**riday   **J**anuary   **S**eptember

2. Capitalize the names of holidays and historical events.

    Christmas   **I**ndependence **D**ay   **W**orld **W**ar I

3. Don't capitalize the names of seasons.

    spring   summer   fall   winter

Titles

1. Capitalize the first word and all important words of titles of books, magazines, newspapers, and articles.

    The Sound and the Fury   *Time Out*

    The New York Times   "The Influence of Hip Hop"

2. Capitalize the first word and all important words of titles of films, plays, radio programs, and TV shows.

    Star Wars   *A Midsummer Night's Dream*

    "All Things Considered"   "Friends"

3. Don't capitalize articles (*a, an, the*), conjunctions (*but, and, or*) and short prepositions (*of, with, in, on, for*) unless they are the first word of a title.

    The Story of Cats   *The Woman in the Dunes*

Appendix 6   Punctuation Rules

Period

1. Use a period at the end of a statement or command.

    I live in New York.   Open the door.

2. Use a period after most abbreviations.

    Ms.   Dr.   St.   U.S.

    Exceptions: NATO   UN   AIDS   IBM

3. Use a period after initials.

    Ms. K.L. Kim   F.C. Simmons

Question Mark

1. Use a question mark at the end of questions.

    Is he working tonight?   Where did they used to work?

2. In a direct quotation, the question mark goes before the quotation marks.

    Martha asked, "What's the name of the street?"

Exclamation Point

Use an exclamation point at the end of exclamatory sentences or phrases. They express surprise or extreme emotion.

    Wow!   I got an A!

Comma

1. Use a comma to separate items in a series.

    John will have juice, coffee, and tea at the party.

2. Use a comma to separate two or more adjectives that each modify the noun alone.

    Purrmaster is a smart, friendly cat. (*smart* and *friendly* cat)

3. Use a comma before a conjunction (*and, but, or, so*) that separates two independent clauses.

    The book is very funny, and the film is funny too.

    She was tired, but she didn't want to go to sleep.

4. Don't use a comma before a conjunction that separates two phrases that aren't complete sentences.

    I worked in a bakery at night and went to class during the day.

    Do you want to see a band or go to a club?

5. Use a comma after an introductory clause or phrase.

> After we hike the first part of the trail, we are going to rest.
>
> If you exercise every day, you will be healthy.

6. Use a comma after *yes* and *no* in answers.

> Yes, that is my book.
>
> No, I'm not.

7. Use a comma to separate nonrestrictive clauses from the rest of a sentence. A nonrestrictive clause gives more information about the noun it describes, but it isn't needed to identify the noun.

> Kevin's new computer, which he needs for work, has a lot of memory.
>
> *Esperanto*, which has Flamenco dancing on Wednesdays, is our favorite restaurant.

8. Use a comma to separate quotations from the rest of a sentence. Don't use a comma if the quotation is a question and it is in the first part of the sentence.

> The student said, "I'm finished with the homework."
>
> "I'm also finished," added his friend.
>
> "Are you really finished?" asked the student.

Apostrophe

1. Use apostrophes in contractions.

> don't (*do not*)   it's (*it is*)   he's (*he is*)   we're (*we are*)

2. Use apostrophes to show possession.

> Anne's book (the book belongs to Anne)

Quotation marks

1. Use quotation marks at the beginning and end of exact quotations. Other punctuation marks go before the end quotation marks.

> Burt asked, "When are we leaving?"
>
> "Right after lunch," Mark replied.

2. Use quotation marks before and after titles of articles, songs, stories, and television shows. Most commonly, periods and commas are placed before the end quotation marks, while question marks and exclamation points are placed after them. If the title is a question, the question mark is placed inside the quotation marks and appropriate punctuation is placed at the end of the sentence.

> Burt's favorite song is "Show Some Emotion" by Joan Armatrading.
>
> He read an article called "Motivating Your Employees."
>
> We read an interesting article called "How Do You Motivate Employees?".

Italics and Underlining

1. If you are writing on a computer, use italic type (*like this*) for books, newspapers, magazines, films, plays, and words from other languages.

   Have you ever read *Woman in the Dunes*?

   The only magazine she reads is *The Economist*.

   How do you say *buenos dias* in Chinese?

2. If you are writing by hand, underline the titles of books, newspapers, magazines, films, and plays.

   Have you ever read <u>Woman in the Dunes</u>?

   The only magazine she reads is <u>The Economist</u>.

   How do you say <u>buenos dias</u> in Chinese?

 # Appendix 7 Writing Basics

1. Sentence types

There are three types of sentences: declarative, interrogative, and exclamatory. Declarative sentences state facts and describe events, people, or things. We use a period at the end of these sentences. Interrogative sentences ask yes/no questions and wh- questions. We use a question mark at the end of these sentences. Exclamatory sentences express surprise or extreme emotion, such as joy or fear. We use an exclamation point at the end of these sentences.

2. Indenting

We indent the first line of a paragraph. Each paragraph expresses a new thought, and indenting helps to mark the beginning of this new thought.

3. Writing titles

The title should give the main idea of a piece of writing. It should be interesting. It goes at the top of the composition and is not usually a complete sentence. In a title, capitalize the first word and all of the important words. Do not capitalize conjunctions (*and, but, so, or*), articles (*a, an, the*), or short prepositions (*at, by, for, in, of, on, out, to, up, with*) unless they are the first word of the title.

4. Writing topic sentences

The topic sentence tells the reader the main idea of the paragraph. It is always a complete sentence with a subject and a verb. It is often the first sentence in a paragraph, but sometimes it is in another position in the paragraph.

5. Organizing ideas

Information can be organized in a paragraph in different ways. One common way is to begin with a general idea and work toward more specific information. Another way is to give the information in order of time using words like *before, after, as, when, while,* and *then*.

6. Connecting ideas

It is important to connect the ideas in a paragraph so that the paragraph has cohesion. Connectors and transitional words help make the writing clear, natural, and easy to read. Connectors and transitional words include *and, in addition, also, so, but, however, for example, such as, so ... that,* and *besides*.

7. The writing process

Success in writing generally follows these basic steps:

- ❖ Brainstorm ideas.
- ❖ Organize the ideas.
- ❖ Write a first draft of the piece.
- ❖ Evaluate and edit the piece for content and form.
- ❖ Rewrite the piece.

Appendix 8   Maps

United States

Canada

ARCTIC OCEAN

ICELAND

GREENLAND

ALASKA

Beaufort Sea

Baffin Bay

Gulf of Alaska

YUKON

NORTHWEST TERRITORIES

NUNAVUT

ATLANTIC OCEAN

PACIFIC OCEAN

BRITISH COLUMBIA

ALBERTA

CANADA

Hudson Bay

NEWFOUNDLAND

SASKATCHEWAN

MANITOBA

QUEBEC

ONTARIO

PRINCE EDWARD ISLAND

NOVA SCOTIA

NEW BRUNSWICK

SCALE

0   1000 Miles

0   1000 KM

UNITED STATES

Asia

Central and South America

Index